YOUR CHILD
AT PLAY

Three to Five Years

YOUR CHILD AT PLAY

Three to Five Years

Conversation, Creativity, and Learning
Letters, Words, and Numbers

SECOND EDITION

MARILYN SEGAL, PH.D.

Foreword by WENDY MASI, PH.D.,
Director of the Family Center at Nova Southeastern University

NEWMARKET PRESS   NEW YORK

To Amelia, Kori, Jennifer, Brenan, Kenneth, Nicholas, Rachel, Gregory, and Peter who are always there to update our knowledge of child play.

A Mailman Family Center Book, published by Newmarket Press, drawn from research conducted at Nova Southeastern University, Ft. Lauderdale, Florida.

This book is published simultaneously in the United States of America and in Canada.

10 9 8 7 6 5 4 3 2 1
Second Edition

Library of Congress Cataloging-in-Publication Data

Segal, Marilyn M.
    Your child at play. Three to five years / Marilyn Segal.—2nd ed.
        p.   cm.
    Includes index.
    ISBN 1-55704-337-X (hc). —ISBN 1-55704-337-7 (pbk.)
        1. Play—United States.   2. Child development—United States.
    I. Title
    HQ782.S426   1998
    155.4'18—DC21   97-49696
                                                       CIP

The author gratefully acknowledges the continuing grant from the A.L. Mailman Family Foundation, Inc., which supported the writing of this book.

QUANTITY PURCHASES
Companies, professional groups, clubs, and other organizations may qualify for special terms when ordering quantities of this title. For information, write to Special Sales, Newmarket Press, 18 East 48th Street, New York, NY 10017; call (212) 832-3575; or fax (212) 832-3629.Credits and acknowledgments of permissions for poetry excerpts are listed on page 284.

Photo credits:

LISA NALVEN PHOTOGRAPHY: pages 1, 3, 4, 6, 7, 9, 16, 18, 22, 23, 25, 27, 33, 40, 43, 45, 50, 54, 55, 58, 61, 64, 65, 67, 68, 70, 71, 73, 78, 81, 88, 89, 92, 94, 97, 100, 101, 102, 104, 107, 108, 109, 110, 113, 116, 118, 123, 126, 129, 130, 135, 138, 144, 145, 147, 160, 166, 171, 175, 176, 178, 187, 188, 192, 196, 197, 201, 208, 210, 219, 222, 227, 233, 235, 238, 240, 241, 243, 246, 247, 249, 254, 261, 262, 264, 275, 276, 278.
BILL SARCHET: pages 30, 119, 140, 142, 156, 158, 162, 193, 204, 216, 220.

Book design by M.J. DiMassi

Acknowledgments

~~~~~~

This book is a collaborative effort.

WENDY MASI, Ph.D., Director of the Family Center at Nova Southeastern University, is my toughest critic. She raked through the manuscript with a fine-tooth comb and weeded out passages that were inaccurate or unclear. Dr. Masi has three delightful children of her own, who just happen to be my grandchildren.

RONI LEIDERMAN, Ph.D., Director of Nova Southeastern University's Family Institute, has years of intimate experience with families of very young children. She and her staff tried out all the suggested activities with parents and babies, and helped me make appropriate changes. She identified cooperative families with adorable children to participate in our photo sessions.

ANN MCELWAIN, M.B.A., Director of Marketing and Product Development at the Family Center at Nova Southeastern University, assumed the major responsibility for implementing the photo sessions. She has an uncanny way of convincing babies to do the right thing at the right time.

SUZANNE GREGORY, my most valuable assistant, has the talent to decipher my handwriting and incorporate volumes of new material and rewrites into a manageable manuscript.

Foreword

~~~~~~

Your Child at Play is a series of books about the joy of playing with your child. When you and your child play together, you are enhancing your child's creativity and imagination, and encouraging flexible thinking. You are also getting back in touch with your own childhood, discovering a playful part of yourself that may have been buried through the years. But most important, you're connecting with your child. You are creating a bond of intimacy that will keep you and your child together in spirit, even through the often stormy teenage years.

The author of this series, Marilyn Segal, is an expert in child development, a noted professor, author, lecturer, researcher, and the founder of Nova Southeastern University's Family Center in Ft. Lauderdale, Florida, devoted to strengthening the family and enhancing the ability of parents and caregivers to nurture children. She is also a mother and grandmother whose heart and soul is invested in children, and believes more than anything in the power of play. Her home is filled with blocks, trains, books, crafts, and dolls, carefully selected so that they will be loved by all her children. Her grandchildren spend hours playing with her dollhouse and Brio set, weaving magical special worlds to which only they and their Nana are privy.

This book series is special because their author is special. She is a five foot, ninety pound powerhouse, who believes that everyone should experience the joy of play, and that playing together is at the heart of every relationship. She is my mother, my mentor, my friend. Her simple message "play together, grow together" is as powerful as it is succinct. Enjoy the books, follow your heart, and you will all have fun.

—Wendi Masi, Ph.D., Director of the Family Center
at Nova Southeastern University

~~~~

Contents

~~~~~~

Introduction

~~~~~~

Rachel, a three-year-old, had a friend over for the afternoon. As usual, Rachel was bossing her friend around and insisting that things be done her way. Rachel's father decided to intervene. "I want you to behave," he told her firmly. "I am being 'have," Rachel countered, and continued to bully her friend.

Like Rachel, children from three to five are taking charge of their own play. Whether they are assigning a task to a peer, investigating the properties of mud and water, or staging a safari in the living room, their play is self-initiated and all-engrossing. The purpose of play is having a good time. The outcome of play is physical, intellectual, and social development.

Your Child at Play is a description of the play behavior of preschool children. It is based on a three-year observational study of children at play in a variety of settings. Its purpose is to describe the diversity and richness of children's play and suggest ways in which parents can foster their children's development by supporting their play ideas.

Your Child at Play is divided into six sections: Playing With Ideas, Active Play, The Scientist at Work, Playing School, Playing With Friends, and Ways of Playing. At the end of each chapter we list suggestions and play ideas that have

~~~~~

been used successfully by other parents.

Your Child at Play is not a textbook that must be read from cover to cover. Turn to the Table of Contents and select a topic that interests you. When you reach the suggestions at the end of the chapters, look for play ideas that you and your child might enjoy. Take into account your own interests as well as the interests of your child. Remember, fun is contagious. Sharing a good time with your child is both your responsibility and your reward.

PLAYING
WITH IDEAS

HOW COME

When the Sun goes down at night,
He paints the sky with colored light.
But when the Moon leaves in the morning,
She sneaks away without a warning.
How come?

When leaves are finished being green,
They put on colors like a queen.
But when flowers wilt and then fall down,
They only turn to just plain brown.
How come?

When Nana was young, her hair was gold.
It turned to silver when she grew old.
My grandpa used to have red hair.
When he got old, he had nothing there.
How come?

—M. Segal

Rachel, a talkative and curious three-year-old, never stops asking questions. "Sometimes they're silly, sometimes they're easy, and sometimes they're questions that even I can't answer," explained Rachel's older sister, Jennifer. Here is the list of questions that Jennifer compiled:

• Why do fairies have funny ears?

• How do tigers go roar?

• Why does your mouth go up when you smile?

• What is it going to do in the world today?

• Why are we people?

5

Preschool children like Rachel are so full of questions that we sometimes find ourselves ignoring them. Yet if we tune into their questions, we can recapture the wonderment of things we otherwise take for granted and recall the naive faith that all questions can be answered. At the same time, we can recognize that questions provide a beautiful opportunity to join in the private world of our child:

Rachel: Why do fairies have funny ears?
Mother: Those kind of ears are very good
for listening to butterfly talk.

Section I describes ways in which children play with ideas by asking questions and engaging their parents in quizzical conversations. In the first chapter, Questions About the World, we look at concepts that are confusing and prompt unexpected questions: When you go in an airplane, do you land on a faraway planet? Are faraway places full of weird animals? Is downtown farther away when it takes longer to get there? In the second chapter we describe how ideas about the past, the present, and the future intrigue and confuse young children. In the third chapter we look at the questions children pose about life itself: Where was I before I was born? How does my body know when it's time to stop growing? What happens to you after you're dead? At the end of each chapter we describe ways of stimulating conversational play that enlightens parents as well as children.

CHAPTER 1

Questions About the World

WINNIE THE POOH

On Monday when the sun is hot,
I wonder to myself a lot.
Now is it true, or is it not,
That what is which, and
Which is what?

—A.A. Milne

As soon as they can crawl, babies show a strong urge to explore new territory, to see what is under the bed or up the stairs. Toddlers, once they have learned to open the front door, may try to walk down the street. Preschool children continue

this pattern. They range farther and farther from home base in their explorations. At the same time, children become aware of even more distant places by taking trips, listening to stories, and watching television. As they talk with their parents about these faraway places, children begin to piece together a larger world.

"Guess what, Daddy?" Nicholas told his father one evening at dinner. "Mama and me saw the Blue Bomber today." (The Blue Bomber is a beat-up jeep owned by Nicholas's uncle.) "It was getting fixed at a gas station on Potato Road."

"But Potato Road is where Uncle Rick lives," Nicholas's dad replied. "I don't think there are any gas stations there."

"Yes," Nicholas insisted, "first we came to Potato Road and then we saw the Blue Bomber getting fixed."

In the past, the Blue Bomber had always been sitting in a driveway at the end of Potato Road. If the Blue Bomber could move, Nicholas reasoned, then so could Potato Road. Nicholas's error is typical of preschool children. It takes a number of years to integrate different bits of spatial information into a reliable map. Nevertheless, preschool children pursue several themes that provide useful information about faraway places. One of these themes is air travel.

FARAWAY PLACES

"When I'm ten," Alberto told his parents very seriously, "I'm going to New York and see the Mets."

"Why wait until you're ten?" his mother wondered.

"Then I'll be old enough to fly on a plane," was the immediate reply.

For many preschool children faraway places seem first and foremost to be places that you get to by airplane. The children

have been attentive to airplanes passing overhead since they were toddlers. Now they understand that these planes bring special guests for visits and then carry them back home. Parents, and perhaps children too, leave on planes for faraway business trips and vacations.

The strong association between air travel and faraway places may lead to the misconception that these places are somewhere up in the air. True, the planes come back down to land, but are they landing on the same surface from which they took off? Without a clear understanding of how points on the earth are interconnected, faraway places may seem like separate worlds:

Kevin: Are there people in the sky?
Mother: I don't think so. Some people think there are people on other planets, but no one has found them.

Kevin: Do people go to the planets?
Mother: They've been to the moon. The planets are too far away.
Kevin: Is California another planet?
Mother: No, it's far away but not as far as the planets.
Kevin: Is Disneyland another planet?
Mother: No, it's in the same state; it's not that far away.
Kevin: Where is the North Pole?
Mother: Way up on top of the world. You have to get there in a plane.
Kevin: Is it in the air?

Interest in air travel stimulates a more advanced understanding of faraway places. Whether or not young children have the opportunity to travel by plane, they become familiar with photographic images of the earth as seen from the air. A highway or city looks much like a road map and the earth actually looks like a globe. Of course, preschool children do not fully comprehend what they are seeing in photographs and television shows. Nevertheless, we should not underestimate the significance of this visual experience. The preschool children of today are used to seeing the world from a perspective that would have dumbfounded adults only a few generations ago.

PRETEND PLACES

Preschool children also associate faraway places with the exotic and unusual. A trip to the zoo, for example, may highlight the fact that many of the animals live far away. Reindeer come from the North Pole, penguins from the South Pole. Kangaroos, elephants, and giraffes live across the ocean. Television shows may give children glimpses of dramatically different weather, geography, and life-styles. Children in the middle of the country are fascinated by characteristics of a coastal environment: volcanoes, snorkeling, surfing, and so on. Conversely, those who live near the ocean are intrigued with inland environments: cattle ranches, huge farms, desserts, and skiing.

The popular story *Where the Wild Things Are*, by Maurice Sendak, presents an image of faraway places that may be similar to one many young children have. Somewhere, far away, lives an incredible assortment of realistic but grotesque animal monsters. They seem to have nothing better to do than gnash their teeth, make horrible growling noises, and wait for children to visit them. Those who are not brave enough to stare the ferocious animals in the face are unlikely to come back. Even as adults, we may have such images in the back of our minds—perhaps a faraway jungle where danger lurks at every step.

Because preschool children do not have a precise way to measure distance, their play may reflect anxiety that unusual animals or types of weather will suddenly turn up. "Don't

KENNETH MASI

worry, George," Jad told his stuffed monkey. "There aren't any wolves around here. They live in the forest." Later Jad's mother saw him open a closet and call for Sharon. "Who's Sharon?" she asked. "That's my pet wolf. I'm going to take her for a walk around the block." Unsure about how far away the forest was, Jad had relieved the tension by creating a harmless "house wolf."

PLACES YOU CANNOT REACH

The most unusual faraway place is outer space. Children are initially drawn to this environment by the technical grandeur of rockets and space shuttles. Space travelers need special suits to provide air and water and to protect them against extreme heat and cold. On a space walk, explorers must be tethered on a rope so they won't float away. As preschool children become aware of these bizarre characteristics of space travel, outer space becomes an exciting place to talk about:

Michael: Rockets took man to the moon, right?
Mother: Right.
Michael: Do rockets go to all the stars in the sky?
Mother: No, stars are like big balls of fire. You can't land on them. You can only land on a solid planet like the earth or the moon.

The remoteness and immensity of outer space makes it hard for preschoolers to imagine. Some preschool children struggle to understand the basic premise that space, tangible though it seems, is out of normal reach:

Dennis: Why can't we touch the sky?
Mother: It's too high.
Dennis: Even if we used a ladder?

ERIC ADCOCK

On the other hand, a child may turn away from the limited reality of space and become absorbed in an outer-space fantasy:

Brenan: Can we go to Mars?
Father: Sure.
Brenan: Then we'll see the Martians and say, "Take us to your leader."
Father: Yeah.
Brenan: I have to tell you one more thing. They're very tricky, right, Daddy? You have to be very careful, there might be a trap door, right, Daddy? If you see a crack, you have to walk in the middle.

Father: Sounds like good advice.
Brenan: Then, if you see a tiger on Mars, you have to watch out.

Faraway places are easier to talk about when children go on a trip, whether by bus, car, train, ship, or airplane. Airplane rides are both fun for and puzzling to preschool children.

When Carina went on an airplane ride her questions were endless: How will the plane get up into the sky? Why do we have to wear belts? Why are the houses getting smaller? How does the airplane know it's not supposed to bump into the moon?

Packing for an airplane trip can be just as exciting as going up in the air. Changes in climate associated with long airplane rides can inspire a host of questions. Why is it hot in Florida when it's going to be cold in New York? Does the sun know how to find New York? Why do I have to dress up in nice clothes when I go to New York? Won't my toys be sad if they can't come on the trip? Could we move to New York so it won't be far away?

The relationship between time and distance is particularly difficult for children. Preschool children do not realize that time is the same when two places share the same longitude, nor do they understand that the seasons become more extreme as latitude increases. They have little if any idea what causes the cycle of day and night or the changes in season. It is a big enough idea to think about daylight coming from faraway places to the east and leaving for faraway places to the west. Parents should not be surprised if their child's thinking about these ideas is more poetic than scientific:

Veronica: The day kills the night.
Mother: What do you mean?
Veronica: The sun comes out and the sun kills the night.

SUGGESTIONS FOR PARENTS

We have outlined several ways that preschool children approach the subject of faraway places. The first thing you as parents can do is to observe which paths your child is most interested in following: Is your child drawn to the fact that faraway places can be reached quickly and dramatically by airplane? Does your child like to talk about where unusual animals, weather, or terrain can be found? Is your child curious about the daily disappearance of the sun? Perhaps he or she is following a path we have not described, for there are many alternatives that lead to the same exciting discoveries.

Whatever path your child seems to prefer, you can enrich his or her adventures along the way. Look for picture books that provide new information. Suppose, for example, that your child keeps asking questions about sharks. This preoccupation suggests that your child would welcome more information about ocean animals. Books with pictures of animals that live in the ocean might lead to longer conversations about faraway places. A child who likes to wear makeup and create flamboyant outfits might be interested in a book that shows jewelry and styles of dress from distant countries.

Even more powerful than photographs are films. Be alert for TV shows that link unusual animals and environments with faraway places. Programs of all kinds, including sports shows and wildlife shows from around the world, provide an immediacy that is difficult to attain in any other way. "Daddy," Suzy blurted out one day. "Do you know where panda bears come from?" "What?" her father mumbled, momentarily confused by the sudden change in their conversation. "From China," Suzy continued triumphantly. "I saw it on 'Sesame Street.'"

By themselves, many programs are not likely to affect preschool children very much. Often the segments are too long and presented with narration children can not follow. Informa-

tion about faraway places may be so mixed with a story line that it does not stand out clearly. Parents can magnify the impact of television by watching shows with their children and commenting on points of interest. They can offer simplified interpretations of complicated narration. Their role as instructor, however, may be a limited one. "Amelia likes to watch 'Heart of the Dragon' (a program about China)," her mother told us. "She doesn't understand the program, but she notices details that interest her, such as the chopsticks, the way people bow to each other, the different-sounding music."

Parents will find opportunities to build on new visual experiences, whether acquired by looking at photographs or watching films, by anchoring them to something more tangible and personal. If your child likes to look at pictures of planes, take him to the airport to see the planes that are constantly coming and going. Seeing a plane pass overhead, a parent might say, "That plane is going south—I think it's going to Grandma's house in Texas. What do you think?" As it is for explorers, it is intriguing for preschool children to imagine heading off in a direction and eventually finding their chosen destination. Try to find aerial photographs of your neighborhood or city. Buy model planes for imaginary trips at home or build a child-size "airplane" with blankets and chairs.

For a child who is interested in the exotic qualities of faraway places, parents can provide experiences that build an awareness of cultural differences. An experience could be as involved as a trip to an authentic Japanese garden in a museum or as simple as hearing the story of the little Dutch boy who put his finger in the dike. A child might enjoy a record of Mid-Eastern belly-dancing music or a doll from Hawaii. Sometimes jigsaw puzzles picture children from different countries. Books are available that tell how holidays are celebrated throughout the world. Trips to different ethnic restaurants provide a fun, informative way to "visit" foreign places.

Perhaps the most natural opportunity for conversing about faraway places is when packing for a trip. The packing process becomes a preview of what is to come and can easily lead to further discussions. Together you can chose clothes according to the climate and activities of the faraway place. If no trip is planned, parents can help children pack for imaginary trips. Imaginary packing extends far beyond the clothes that will be needed. A child planning a mountain-climbing expedition will certainly need a snack for quick energy, binoculars for watching mountain sheep, and a shortwave radio for sending emergency messages.

By the end of the preschool period, most children realize that in some ways places are represented on a map. Pointing to a particular shape on the map, the children proudly announce its name, much as they used to label pictures in a book. The relationships between the shapes are subject to gross miscalculation:

Pierre: Which way is Miami?
Mother: That way.
Pierre: Is Miami near Nevada?
Mother: Gosh, remember on the map? It's here on the other side of the map.
Pierre: Yeah, that's right.

Despite such confusion, children benefit from this rote learning. Being able to name some faraway places on a map sets the stage for later understanding of spatial relationships, just as rote counting stimulates children to begin counting objects. Parents who like to make toys can make a homemade map puzzle by putting a cardboard backing on a map of their own area. As the child puts the puzzle together, perhaps with the parents' help, it will give the parents a chance to talk about locations that have meaningful associations for the child.

In order to get beyond rote learning, parents can draw simple route maps. The map might show the way to a friend's house, indicating right and left turns and several landmarks. Later on, a parent might draw a larger map consisting of major highways in a city, including nearby towns that are familiar to the child. Many parents find they can reduce a child's restlessness during a car trip by talking about landmarks that are coming up. Drawing route maps is an extension of this idea.

As children become interested in the spatial relationships between faraway places, parents can look for opportunities to introduce new information about distance and direction. Questions about the disappearance of the sun, for example, may lead

to a talk about east and west. The term "north" might be introduced when discussing the location of Santa Claus. New information about distance can be expressed in terms that are within the understanding of the child. For a child who is just becoming aware of the magnitude of the number one hundred, parents might say, "Hawaii is more than a hundred miles away." For more advanced counters, parents could say, "many hundreds of miles, more than a thousand miles," or "about three thousand miles."

When preschool children are particularly interested in faraway places, playing with a globe is appropriate. Having found where they live, the children enjoy locating the country that is on the opposite side of the globe. Vague notions about the other side of the world become more precise when linked with time: When it is noon here, it is midnight there. When we get up, they are having dinner. What do you think they are doing when you go to bed? Children who become fascinated with this game of global opposites will be interested in the relationship between hemispheres and seasons. Faraway places in the Southern Hemisphere (the bottom of the globe) have opposite seasons from those in the United States. When it's Christmas weather here, they have Fourth of July weather there. When the leaves come out on our trees, they are falling off of the trees there.

Faraway places are a topic of fascination to preschool children. The impetus to explore this new frontier may be a trip or someone coming for a visit. In fact, faraway places are often identified with specific individuals: "California is where Uncle Joshua lives." Other times, faraway places are discovered by accident. The child sees something unusual or frightening, asks questions, and discovers the existence of a faraway place.

Conversations with children about faraway places spurs their curiosity and excites their imagination. They recognize that there are different kinds of far away places: places where friendly people live, places where strange animals live, and places you can talk about but never, never visit.

PLAY IDEAS

Follow your child's interests. You might help your child make an ocean mural by pasting stickers, magazine pictures, or her own drawings on a blue background. If your child is interested in hats, look at pictures in a natural history or geography magazine or children's encyclopedia together. Talk about all the different hats you can find that people wear in different places for special jobs or special occasions.

Show your preschooler a photo album from a trip you took. Talk about where your family went and what kinds of things you saw.

While your preschooler is watches, draw a map that goes from your front door to the bedroom. Walk along the path with your child and let him find the lines on the paper that relate to the walk he is taking. Perhaps he will recognize that maps help you find out how to get where you are going.

Keep a diary of the questions your child asks. Does she ask more sophisticated questions as she grows older?

Show your preschooler a videotape of another country. Talk about how the people dress, what they eat, and what they are doing.

Read a book like *Oh, the Places You'll Go* by Dr. Seuss or *Where the Wild Things Are* by Maurice Sendak. Help your child draw a pretend animal who lives in a faraway place.

CHAPTER 2

What Is, What Was, and What Will Be

~~~~~~~~~~~~~~~~~~~~~~~~~~~~~~~~~

As Tommy Snooks and Bessy Brooks
Were walking out one Sunday,
Says Tommy Snooks and Bessy Brooks,
Tomorrow will be Monday.

Oliver: Is today the day we go on the airplane?
Dad: No, ten more days.
Oliver: I'm going on an airplane when I'm four, right?
Dad: That's right, we're going to visit Grandpa in Minnesota and feed his cows.
Oliver: And when I'm five, I'll ride a school bus to kindergarten.

Nearly every morning Travis and his father have a similar conversation. Travis is interested in talking about his plans for the future. The problem is that he is not sure when the future will arrive. The concept of time, like faraway places or the life process, is a mystery to preschool children. By asking questions, however, children like Travis can gradually build a framework for measuring the future.

Time stretches out in both a forward and backward direction. Children's awareness of how time expands, however, is not symmetrical. A one- or two-year-old is much better at talking about the past than about the future. By the beginning of the preschool years, the child's notion of the past is filled with specific experiences that can be recounted in conversation. The future, on the other hand, is largely empty. Like Oliver's air-

~~~

plane trip and school bus ride, a few signposts exist in an otherwise uncharted territory. By the end of the preschool years, as we will see in this chapter, the future has become an approachable topic of conversation. Being able to anticipate the future, the children can now enjoy it more fully.

WHAT WAS

Preschool children may sound surprisingly sophisticated when referring to the recent past. At the dinner table one night, Faria turned to her mother and remarked, "You haven't made that dish for a while." By the same token, children can recount the past to the point of tedium. "Mom, guess what?" Debbie began. "Today at school we had a parade, and I colored my hat with a red-and-blue crayon. I made the stripes going up this

way. Then we put on our hats and we made a line outside the door. I held Alexis's hand. We went downstairs . . ."

Whether they are being clever or tiresome, preschoolers' ability to make sense out of the past is impressive. When children begin to describe future events, it is understandable that they are most likely to talk about experiences that parallel those from the past. Davita, spotting some pumpkins on a roadside stand, remembered Halloween. "When is Halloween coming back?" she asked. Carina, after looking at photos of her last birthday party, began to plan her next one. Once children have organized the past, the future becomes much clearer.

"Nicholas, are you going to school Monday?" his grandmother asked.

"No, I can't," Nicholas explained, "'cause we already had the last-day-of-school party."

THE HERE AND NOW

"I want to watch 'Sesame Street,'" Bertram insisted. "But you can't," his mother countered. "It doesn't begin until after dinner." "I want to watch television now," Bertram insisted again.

For children like Bertram, the present is that very minute. Sometime this month and this year has no meaning for them. If "Sesame Street" is showing "today," it has to be showing that very minute. "I go to preschool," means "I am on the way to preschool right now."

It takes a long time for preschool children to learn about the present. Bertram's aunt asked if a neighbor still lived in the house beside them. "No," Bertram explained. "Mr. Wilson is working."

Talking about what is happening is more difficult than talking about what has already happened. When her father suggested that it was a good day for sledding, Allison wanted to leave the house immediately. "Today" and "right now" meant the same thing as far as Allison was concerned. Thomas was even more puzzled than Allison when his teacher told him it was the first day of spring. "It can't be spring," Thomas explained, "the flowers aren't starting to grow." Like most preschoolers, Thomas could not grasp the concept of a calendrical season. Seasons, as far as he was concerned, were not related to the months of the year. Winter was when the snow came. Spring was when the flowers grew.

LOOKING FORWARD

Conversations about the future presuppose some system for measuring time. By three years of age, most children have a working knowledge of terms that refer to a vague but not distant future, terms like "next," "later," and "soon." They may even be using these terms to ask about the family's daily plans. Three-year-olds also have some understanding of the word "tomorrow." Tomorrow, however, is a term whose precise meaning is hard to capture because it keeps turning into today:

Erik: When is tomorrow?

Mother: When you wake up in the morning, it will be tomorrow; but when it happens, it will be today.

Erik: Is it ever going to be tomorrow?

As preschool children become more interested in the future, they need terms that are not as limited as "tomorrow" or as vague as "later" and "soon." Parents start referring to days of the week, and gradually children become familiar with these special words. Some three-year-olds can actually recite all the names in order. More often, preschool children focus on learning the names of days that are special to them. Jad, like many children, organized his week around a favorite television show. "Is 'Mr. Roger's Neighborhood' on today?" he kept asking his mother. "Not until Friday—that's three more days," she would respond. Other preschool children distinguish between the days they go to school and the days they don't. Michael referred to Monday, Wednesday, and Friday as "up" days, because he got up and went to school.

In the process of identifying special days of the week, the children gain a feeling for the week's length. When "Mr.

Roger's Neighborhood" ends, they have to wait a whole long time before it comes back on again. This is a difficult concept for three- or four-year-olds who assume that television shows are at the beck and call of the viewer. Similarly, weekends, with their promise of a trip to the beach or lunch at McDonald's, are a week apart. Developing a crude notion of a week gives preschool children a useful unit of time. Phrases like "next week" or "in a week" signify that an event is a few days away, but are not so far in the future that they never happen.

The week as a unit of time is tied to the near future. As adults, we rarely think in aggregates larger than six to eight weeks. For us, the month is the unit related to more distant events. For preschool children, however, months have little meaning. As their attention focuses on units of time larger than a week, the future is organized around upcoming holidays and seasonal changes.

In fact, the four seasons seem to be blended with holidays to form a calendar of holiday seasons. Fall, Halloween, and Thanksgiving combine to form a holiday season in which there is a grand mixture of turkey, pumpkins, witches, and colored leaves swirling down the block. Then comes the winter season with its festive religious holidays, followed by the spring holiday season, and finally the summer/Fourth of July season. Sandwiched in between are minor holidays like Valentine's Day and Lincoln's Birthday. And in addition, of course, there are personal holidays in every family: birthdays, vacations, and other special occasions.

Preschool children vary in their holiday preferences, and parents differ in their manner of celebrating them. However, when the schools, stores, and television programs feature a holiday, preschool children are bound to be caught up in whatever event is approaching. Naturally, children try to pinpoint the date. Not having a reliable system that extends beyond a week, their initial estimates may seem ludicrous:

Kevin: When I wake up will it be Christmas?
Mother: No, it won't be Christmas for a couple of weeks.
Kevin (three months later): Will next Tuesday be Valentine's, too?
Mother: No, it won't. Valentine's comes only once a year.

With the help of such conversations, many preschool children progress to the point when they can accurately anticipate a holiday two or three weeks in advance.

THE YEARS AHEAD

The cycle of holidays is completed in one year, and many preschool children are interested in talking about this cycle. However, they usually remember the sequence of only two or three holidays. A more meaningful marker for a year is their birthday, when they will be one year older. For a four-year-old, "next year" means "when I'm five."

This personalized system for measuring years makes it difficult for children to think about age differences. Nicholas wondered if he was still older than his cousin, Elizabeth. He had been four and she had been three, but now, since her birthday, they both were four. This kind of relationship is easier to sort out when children are a couple of years apart in age. "I'll always be older than Sing-Lu," four-year-old Chen exclaimed with satisfaction. He had figured out that his one-year-old brother might gain on him at times, but he would never catch up. If the children try to think about large differences in age, chances are they will get completely lost. Michael, for example, asked his mother, "Were you older than me when I was born?"

In thinking about the years ahead, preschool children have learned that growing older will also mean growing bigger. When they find that the correlation between age and size is not consistent, they are puzzled:

Michael (referring to an old lady who was riding in the car): Is she a big lady?
Mother: No, she is small.
Michael: She can't be small if she's old. Is Daddy bigger than Nana?
Mother: Daddy's bigger, but Nana's older.

Obviously, it is difficult for preschool children to project themselves years into the future. Imagining a job or career is a difficult task. The children do, however, become aware that adults earn money from their jobs, and they may want to discuss what they will buy when they grow up. Alberto told his Daddy that when he got big and made lots of money he was going to buy "a robot, and a big, big box of crayons with points, and a new car that don't got a flat tire."

As you will see in Chapter 3, many children think of growing up as having a baby and being a parent. Having a baby is often associated with getting married, and this aspect of adulthood may trouble preschool children. They ask their parents whom they are going to marry. When their parents say they don't know, children try out some suggestions. They may suggest marrying cousins, friends of the same sex, or parents, only to find out that their parents won't condone any of these choices. In effect, the children are left with the unappetizing probability that they will marry a stranger. In addition, the prospect of marriage implies separation from the only family they know. Children cannot imagine wanting to move away from their parents:

Kevin: When I'm married, I'll still live in the same house with you, right?
Mother: If you want to, you and your wife can live here. But when you're married you have your own family and will like to have your own house.
Kevin: But I don't want my own family. I just want you and Daddy.

The grade-school and high-school years are nearer and clearer to children. They may be interested in talking about the schools they will attend, or they might ask questions about privileges they are looking forward to. A major theme in these conversations is increased physical freedom. Preschool children like to talk about being able to walk to school by themselves or ride their bikes in the neighborhood to visit friends and stores on their own.

The pinnacle of physical freedom seems to reside in driving. Not only do the children fantasize about the vehicles they will drive, they engage in considerable backseat driving. In fact, their questions and directives while riding in the car suggest that they envision being allowed to drive in the near future. They comment about stoplights and turn arrows, speed limits and one-way signs, lane markers and center lines:

Kori: Are we going to go on the bumpy road?
Mother: You mean the road with speed bumps?
Kori: Yeah.
Mother: No, we're not going that way.
Kori: Well, don't go the way where the end died.
Mother: No, we aren't going down a dead-end street.

From all these conversations about the years ahead, preschool children begin to divide their own lifespan into rough age categories. They will be big children, teenagers, and then adults. Adulthood tends to be an undifferentiated period from the mid-twenties to old age. Preschool children with teenage siblings know that first you are a teenager and then you are an

adult. Children who have frequent contact with elderly relatives or neighbors may have a separate category for old people. It is hard for children to think about the life cycle. Even one or two years into the future is a long time when compared with next week or the next holiday.

As adults, we sometimes enter the land of wishes when thinking about the future. It is interesting, however, that conversations about the future between parents and preschool children tend to be on the realistic side. Children focus on the near future, and their aim is to identify what is really going to happen, what is really possible. Behind their attempts to talk about the future, there seems to be a message about autonomy: "Help me predict the future, so I can feel more in control."

SUGGESTIONS FOR PARENTS

One of the curious characteristics of early memory is that children's most vivid memories tend to be negative rather than positive. As a three-year-old, Jennifer recalled a vacation to Hawaii her family had taken when she was two years old. What she remembered was a string of, from her viewpoint, misfortunes. Her doll's shoe got lost, the statue of a donkey near her room had a broken leg, and one morning her father couldn't get a newspaper at breakfast.

Although what is a calamity to a child may be trivial to an adult, children need opportunities to talk about past misfortunes. Bringing these memories into the light of conversation will reduce their intensity. You can also use these memories as a springboard to discuss the future. Jennifer's parents, for example, might ask her what she would do, now that she is four years old, if her doll's shoe got lost on vacation.

When encouraging your preschool child to talk about the future, start from something basic. Remember that preschoolers are just beginning to use language in this way. A first step might be to associate the idea of counting with the future. If your child asks when a particular event will occur, you can respond by telling her the number of days remaining. As children show interest in learning the concept of a week, parents can emphasize that a week is seven days. A simple linear calendar might be made, indicating the seven days of the week and the special events that will occur that week.

More advanced calendars can be introduced as children show the ability to anticipate a period longer than a week. You can try a pad calendar. Write a single number on each page of the pad, starting with the number of days remaining until a holiday and then decreasing to zero (for example: twenty days until Halloween, nineteen days, etc.). An alternative would be to lengthen the simple weekly calendar and label the squares with the days of the month, from the first to the holiday (February 1, 2 . . . 14—Valentine's Day). A third possibility, which is fun for children who can read numerals, is to make a special holiday calendar: Draw a large simple symbol for the holiday, such as an Easter egg for Easter, onto poster board. On the Easter egg, cut out a U-shaped flap, like a window, for each day of the month before the holiday. Glue smaller pictures (simple drawings, like flowers, are fine) behind the windows so that the pictures can be seen when the windows are opened. Finally, write a date on each of the windows. As each day comes, the child can search for the date and open the window to see the picture.

Eventually, some preschool children show interest in the standard calendar. However, these calendars are too confusing for most preschool children because they include both a horizontal and vertical pattern. The calendars we have suggested are much simpler, and they are designed to highlight the special days that preschool children use to measure the future. Moreover, these homemade calendars allow at least a limited amount of handling. Children get to tear a page off the pad calendar, fold and unfold a linear calendar, or peek inside the windows of a holiday calendar.

PLAY IDEAS

Reading books with young children is an ideal pre-holiday activity, but don't limit yourself to books about the holiday. For Christmas, Chinese New Year, Chanukah, Kwanzaa, or Las Posadas, you can read books about winter, books about candles, or books about going shopping. Easter reading can be extended by reading books about bunnies, spring flowers, birds that lay eggs, or even a book about parades. If your child has a large collection of books she might enjoy sorting some of them

by holiday season. Then she can pick stories according to her mood. It will not be surprising if she thinks about Christmas during the middle of the summer or wishes to read a story about a summer picnic during a winter storm.

You and your child can "read" photo albums, looking at the pictures of past holidays and birthdays. Again, if a family has many pictures they can create separate albums for different holidays. An Easter album, for example, would show the family's celebration of that holiday, year by year. You can make holiday-season books for your child using drawings and magazine pictures. The theme of a book might be "What we will do at Kwanzaa," or "Things we like about winter."

As adults, we know that anticipation is translated into mental images of what we hope will happen. Preschool children like to act out their mental images by pretending. Part of your preparation for a holiday can be the creation of props for pretend celebrating. At Christmas or Chanukah, for example, your child may want to handle the presents long before it is time to open them. One possible solution is to wrap up some pretend presents, which can be opened and refilled as part of your child's play. There can be pretend Easter eggs (such as painted rocks) for mock hunts, dress-up clothes for experimenting with different Halloween costumes, pretend party favors for a birthday party, and so on.

Pretending is not limited to the period preceding a special occasion. Halloween costumes are good all year round, and your child may even want to pretend it's time for trick-or-treating. The same is true for pretending that it is Christmas Eve and Santa Claus is visiting. One way to support these imaginary holiday seasons is to save old greeting cards and help your child decorate the house with them.

Of course, many conversational possibilities exist when you and your child explore what will happen during a holiday. Early in the holiday season, conversations center around preparations: the making of decorations for the house, the buying of presents, special baking and cooking projects. Later conversations focus on the sequence of events that will take place during the actual holiday:

Arianna:Will the Easter Bunny come when I'm still sleeping?
Mother:That's what he did last year.
Arianna: If I'm waked up, will he still come?
Mother: Easter Bunnies are very shy. If you think you hear his footsteps, close your eyes really tight.
Arianna:And then can I go find the Easter eggs?
Mother:Yes, right after you eat your breakfast.

Then, after the holiday, there are conversations about how the next holiday will be different. Having just learned about one holiday, preschool children often assume that the next holiday is going to be similar. After Halloween, Kevin wondered what kind of costume he would wear for Christmas. Cynthia expected the Christmas tree to be followed by an Easter tree. Finding out that the next holiday is altogether different makes the future even more exciting.

At the end of the day, talk to your preschooler about the things he did. Help him remember the details that captured his interest. Ask him to guess what is going to happen tomorrow.

Gather props for a holiday such as Las Posadas, Halloween, or a birthday. Pretend you are celebrating the holiday. Talk about when you will really celebrate the holiday that you played celebrating.

Create a weekly calendar for your child out of train shapes for each day of the week and glue magnets to the backs. Let him add a new car every day until he has completed the week. Putting the train on the refrigerator usually works quite well.

Read a book to your child about a holiday that is not too far away. Every day explain to your child that the holiday is getting closer.

CHAPTER 3

Questions About Life

~~~~~~

THE QUESTIONS

When you water plants, it helps them grow.
Does it work with people? I don't know.
When I was as tiny as could be,
Did Mom take a drink and water me?
If I eat my food, will I grow tall?
But what if I don't eat it all?
When I'm a Mom, will I keep growing?
Will something make my growth start slowing?
When I am old as old can be,
Will I look like Grandma, or like me?

Children, from a very young age, are curious about the properties of living things. How are people born? What makes people grow bigger, and what makes them stop growing when they are big? What does it feel like to die, and what happens to you when you are dead? Unfortunately, there are no pat answers to these questions, and parents often find themselves unprepared for the kinds of questions they are asked. In this chapter we describe conversations about the life process: being born, growing, and dying.

When Allison accompanied her mother to the obstetrician, the nurse let her listen to the baby's heartbeat. As soon as the nurse left the room, Allison questioned her mother,

"Mommy, when I listen to the baby with that thing does she hear me back?"

Like Allison, preschool children are beginning to discover some of the properties of life. They know that being alive means hearing, feeling, seeing, talking, and being able to move. They are aware of life around them and are attracted to things that change. On an intuitive level, at least, young children know the difference between animate and inanimate objects. A child who has just learned to walk will step on a stone and walk around a turtle.

Understanding the properties of life is not an easy task. Life means changes that are both gradual and sudden, short-term and long-term. Life means a beginning and an end. As adults we are accustomed to these changes. For preschool children, growth, birth, and death are new discoveries. As they investigate the properties of life, young children are confronted with its essential mystery.

BIRTH

"Mommy, did that baby come out of your tummy? Could you put him back?"

Birth is not a secretive process in our society, and children become aware of it quite early. Even if their own mothers are not pregnant with future sisters and brothers, children soon notice pregnant women. Pregnancy is announced with special clothes, sustained with exercise classes, and often culminates in a well-photographed finale. Parents generally feel comfortable answering their children's questions about pregnancy by telling them that a new baby is growing inside the mother. If children have the opportunity, they enjoy feeling the movement of the developing baby, and they may ask further questions about life inside the uterus: How does the baby eat? Is the baby sleepy now? Does the baby love me? When you take a drink of water does the baby get wet?

Preschool children are particularly curious about how the baby will get out. Judging the baby to be about the size of the mother's belly, it must seem like an impossible feat. Allison's mother explained that the baby is in a special place called the uterus. When the baby is ready to be born it is pushed out of the uterus and comes out through the vagina. Allison continued to ask questions: "Mommy, was the baby in your tummy always there and then it grew bigger? Did you eat a little seed and it grew to be a baby? How come the baby didn't fall out of the opening when it was still little? Is there a baby in my tummy? Why not? Is Daddy growing a baby in his tummy?" "No, mommies grow babies, but daddies get them started." Fortunately for Allison's mother, Allison got tired of this confusing conversation and asked for some chocolate milk.

When children continue to ask questions about birth, parents struggle to find answers. Some parents solve the problem by becoming more descriptive. Other parents find it awkward to acknowledge their child's curiosity, and then confess that some questions are hard to answer. Fortunately, preschool children are not likely to pursue a conversation when they don't get answers that they can understand.

Katie, at five years old, explained the birth process to her grandmother. "Babies start out as a spot in their Mommy's tummy. The spot starts to get bigger and bigger and bigger. Then the spot turns into a baby and it makes her mother's skin stretch. Then her mommy's tummy gets so big that her skin can't stretch anymore. The mommy goes to the hospital and her baby gets borned."

A second line of questioning that children are likely to pursue concerns the way generations are linked. Other children keep bombarding their family with questions. Brenan uncovered this connection by accident:

Brenan: You've got someone growing in your stomach, right, Nana?
Nana: No, not now.
Brenan: But you did have, right?
Nana: Yes, a long time ago, I had my babies a long time ago.
Brenan: What happened to them? They died, right?
Nana: No, they grew up.
Brenan: Where are they?
Nana: Well, your Mommy's right here, and my other baby, your Uncle Vincent, is in California.

Children notice that Grandpa and Grandma are also called Mom and Dad. They hear stories and see pictures of their parents as children. Struggling to make sense out of this new information, the children often repeat what parents tell them.

"My Grandma is your mother," Faria intoned solemnly, as if asking her parents for confirmation. "Are you talking about your mother or my mother?" she teased when she overheard her parents discussing Grandma. Later she surprised Grandma by asking, "Where are your Mom and Dad?"

Brenan, who at first did not know Nana was a mother, subsequently realized she also had been a baby:

Brenan: Nana wasn't always alive.
Mother: That's right. Nana was conceived in her mother's stomach, and she was born to her mother.
Brenan: Well, her mother wasn't always alive.
Mother: Yes, she was conceived. Her name was Mama Cecina, but she's dead now.

Continuing the conversation, Brenan showed there were limits to his new insight:

Brenan: Gorillas weren't never alive.
Mother: Yes, they were conceived also.

Brenan: Was King Kong conceived?
Mother: Yes, he was a baby gorilla once.
Brenan: No, he was always King Kong.

Preschool children inevitably reach a limit when they keep trying to extend the generational sequence back in time. Rosita asked her mother how the first person in the world had a baby. Fabian asked who was born before anybody else. Cynthia wondered who "made God alive." There are no easy answers to these questions. We can appreciate Kenneth's bewilderment when his older sister tried to explain evolution to him. Turning to his father he asked in disbelief, "Was Great-Grandmother ever a monkey?"

A third birth theme that preschool children try to understand concerns the period before their own conception. The subject may arise innocently when parents and children are talking about events in the past:

Nicholas: Where was I when you lived in Hawaii?
Mother: You weren't born yet.
Nicholas: But where was I?

Like Nicholas, most preschool children will not accept the idea of nonexistence. Parents who tell their children that they were with God before they were born are likely to be asked who God is. Is God a different father or mother? Did they live with a different family and in a different place? Unable to believe that they belonged to another family, children may conclude that they were always inside their mother. "I was just very, very, very tiny," Amelia explained to her parents, "and then got bigger." Danny's mother, who was being driven to distraction by his questions, told Danny that he had been in her thoughts. Danny, completely confused by this answer, stopped asking questions.

Although a young child's interest in birth most often takes the form of a conversation with parents, birth themes are also evident in imaginative play. Children whose mothers are pregnant are especially prone to act out the sequence of prenatal growth and delivery. When Jennifer's mother was pregnant, Jennifer lined up all her stuffed animals. Using a stethoscope to listen to their stomachs, she spoke to each animal in turn: "Camel, you have a baby camel in your tummy . . . Pooh Bear, you have a baby Pooh . . . Curious George, you have a baby George . . . ."

GROWING

Being alive means that between birth and death you will grow. Since the process of growth is imperceptible, preschool children are especially interested in body parts that grow or change rapidly. Hair is a prominent example of growth. On top of the head, it grows quickly enough to necessitate periodic trimming. On a man's chin, it needs to be shaved daily. Children often cry when they get their hair cut and are sure that it's going to hurt. Although hair clearly grows, it also falls out. In fact, so much may fall out that a grown-up becomes bald. The body hair of parents is distributed in a dramatic pattern. They have hair under their arms, pubic hair, and perhaps hair on their chests. Preschool children notice these peculiarities of hair, and they wonder about its unpredictable growth. Will they have hairy legs someday? How long will their hair grow if it is not cut? Could a person grow as much body hair as a shaggy dog?

Skin is another part that grows almost fast enough to watch. New skin can be seen under a scab or blister. Cuts are sealed as if by magic. Just as the growth of hair changes with age, so does skin. The skin of teenagers and adults develops imperfections such as moles, freckles, and pimples. Very old people's skin grows in wrinkles and that's why they look sort of funny. Again, preschool children notice these patterns. They marvel at the body's ability to build skin, and they wonder when their skin will change.

Children who are especially interested in hair may express this interest in their pretend play. Allison loved to brush her doll's hair, mess it up, and then start over again. "Molly, stay still. I am brushing your hair. Oh, you got it all messed up. I have to brush it again." Peter insisted on taking out his play razor every time his father shaved. "You and me are shaving," he told his father, "'cause we want to look nice."

Children who are interested in skin are also likely to experiment with make-up. Mason came out of the bathroom with lipstick all over his face. "Mason, what have you been up to now?" his mother asked. "I got to look nice because I am going to Grandma's." Jennifer's way of making herself pretty was to draw pictures on her arm with felt-tipped magic markers. "I made my hands all pretty and red," she boasted to her mother. "You like it, Mommy?"

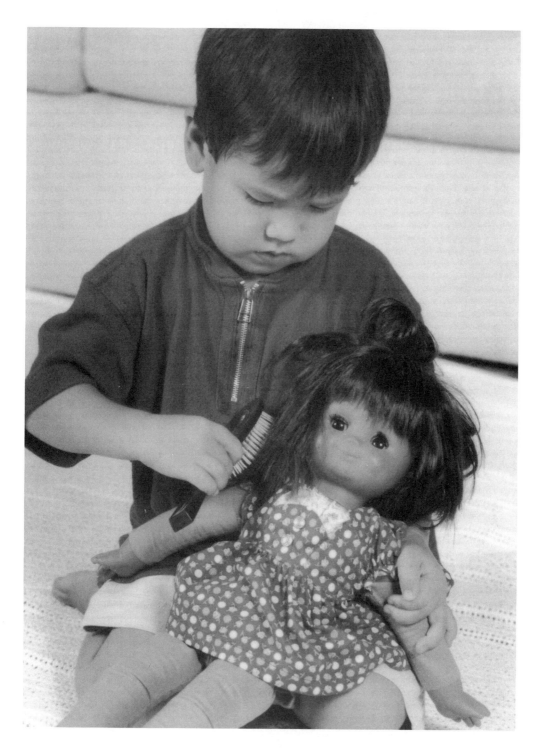

Sometimes preschool children wonder about growing bigger. Typically parents assure them that if they eat the right foods, they will grow. Although the children usually do not take to heart these lectures about nutrition, they do accept the idea that eating will lead to growth. Still, the end point of growth is unclear. Dennis seemed to assume that he would grow into a giant:

Dennis:When I get older, will I grow out of this house?
Mother:What do you mean? Will you get too tall for it?
Dennis:Will I be tall and go through the ceiling?

Other children figure out a reverse pattern. People first grow bigger and then grow smaller again. Children may think that the end point of growth is a matter of choice. Parents can explain that adults stop growing taller (although not heavier or stronger), but it is difficult for preschool children to see so far into the future. Frequently, their understanding of growth is based more on their wishes than on biological facts.

DYING

Just as being alive means you were born, it also means you will die. Parents are understandably reluctant to expose preschool children to death. However, children discover it anyway, even if no close relative dies during the preschool years. Death is all around us. Bugs are killed without a second thought and meat from dead animals is served at the family table. Pets, whose life expectancies are short, often die while children are still young. Above all else, death, both feigned and real, appears on television.

Preschool children ask questions about these different manifestations of death, but the focus of their concern is quite personal. When Arianna's grandfather died, she asked her mother if Grandma was going to die too. Faria, after seeing a program about a single mother, assumed that her dad was going to die. "Mommy," she asked, "will I get a new dad when Daddy dies?" When Yoko's dog died, Yoko's first concern was about her own death. "Mommy, will you get another daughter when I die?"

In attempting to quiet their children's anxiety about death, parents often link death with old age. They admit that the children, and other family members, will die, but they stress that it will not happen for a long time. Many parents explain death as occurring because our bodies wear out.

On the surface, this approach relieves children, and their questions usually stop for the time being. Beneath the surface, children seem to remain troubled about death, for the issue periodically arises. One sign of continued concern is a child's attempts to find an exception to the universality of death. In the following conversation, it is not hard to see Jerome's hope that perhaps, just perhaps, it is possible to escape death:

Jerome: Will Joe the barber get dead?
Dad: Yes.
Jerome: Will the church guy?
Dad: You mean the priest? Yes, he will die too.
Jerome: The whole neighborhood's going to get dead?
Dad: Yes.
Jerome: Even Mickey Mouse?

Questions about what happens after death are another sign that children are looking more closely into this subject. Initially, the children may be curious about funerals and how we dispose of dead bodies. The existence of cemeteries, where a seemingly endless number of dead people are buried, can come as quite a surprise. Thinking further about the idea of being buried, the children begin to realize the physical consequences of death:

Kevin: Are you happy when you're dead?
Mother: No.
Kevin: Are you sad?
Mother: No, you don't feel anything.
Kevin: Do you move when you die?
Mother: No.
Kevin: Can you play when you're dead?
Mother: No, you can't do anything.

Parents who believe in an afterlife would answer Kevin's questions somewhat differently, of course. However, even then children sense that physical existence as they have known it will cease. Whatever heaven may be like, it does not seem worth an immediate visit:

Veronica: How do people get down from God?
Mother: Well, they don't want to come down. It's so beautiful up there. They love it.
Veronica: I don't want to go up to heaven.
Mother: I don't want you to, either.
Veronica: I don't want you to go up.
Mother: Well, I don't plan to go soon.

Children eventually recognize flaws or incomplete responses in their parents' explanations of death and want to pursue the topic further. They realize that death is not restricted to old age but can be caused by many dangerous situations. Car accidents, for example, are a life-threatening danger that parents talk a lot about while they drive. Preschool children are attentive to such comments and often want to converse about car accidents they observe along the road.

Many preschool children are also very sensitive to the danger of being attacked by an animal. These dangerous creatures range from everyday acquaintances—bumblebees, spiders, and neighborhood dogs—to exotic animals such as lions, tigers, and crocodiles, and on to completely imaginary monsters, witches, and giants. In their questions, the children often try to clarify the whereabouts of a dangerous creature. Relatively familiar bees and spiders have a habit of appearing unexpectedly; who knows when a crocodile or giant might show up?

Life-threatening dangers, like car accidents and animal attacks, are a recurrent theme in the imaginative play of preschool children. "Watch out," Michael told Suzy as they swung together. "There's alligators down there." The two friends liked to pretend that they were swinging over an alligator pit. "Ooh, I fell in," yelled Suzy, rolling on the ground. Lying still, she announced, "I'm dead." "I'll make you come alive," Michael assured her as he pointed his finger at her and made a high-pitched "laser" sound.

In imaginative play, sudden death is matched by sudden resurrection. This reversibility undoubtedly helps children cope with their discovery of death. At the same time, it alerts us to the fact that they are becoming aware of and anxious about the permanence of death.

Life is perilous in many ways, and preschool children can become worried about other dangers, such as hurricanes, earthquakes, fire, or kidnapping. In each instance, they explore, through conversation and play, possible deviations from a "normal" death in old age. Usually the prospect of a premature death does not terrify them, but it is nevertheless a real and unresolved concern for a period of time.

In this chapter we have discussed some of the mysteries that preschool children discover as they talk about what it means to be alive. They learn that all people were once babies who grew inside their mothers. They have some understanding

of how families are continued from one generation to the next and when it will be their turn to be parents. They know that everyone must die, and they are aware that death can be caused by many dangers. They know that they are growing, and they have learned about some of the ways their bodies will change with age.

Finding out what it means to be alive is a serious business with preschool children. The questions they ask parents are truly matters of life and death. As parents seek out appropriate answers to their children's persistent questioning, they find themselves walking a tightrope. On the one hand, they want to be truthful with their children and provide answers that are credible. On the other hand, they don't want their children to get anxious or confused. For every one of us, the time comes when we have to admit to our children that although we are perfectly willing to talk, we don't know all the answers.

SUGGESTIONS FOR PARENTS

When children become curious about birth, death, or growth, parents can enrich conversations by providing relevant experiences. Opportunities to touch and play with a newborn baby, photographs of family members as babies, and mementoes from a child's infancy will stimulate further conversations about birth. Reading a children's story about death or visiting a cemetery can help answer a child's questions about death. Planting a garden or taking care of a baby animal highlights the process of growth.

The most difficult conversations occur when preschool children lose a close friend or relative through death. In their desire to comfort children, parents may talk about death as being like sleep. They may refer to the dead person as resting, or being at peace. As well meaning as these phrases are, they can further frighten young children, for they link death with relaxation and going to sleep. A better approach is to emphasize that a dead person does not hurt in any way.

The child's grief centers on the fact that death means separation. Parents can try to direct conversations toward pleasant memories, for this is a link we still have with those who have died. Remembering is facilitated by giving the child a photograph of the dead person, or something that belonged to him or her. Even the funeral can be remembered in a positive way: the fancy coffin, the bright flowers, the natural beauty of the cemetery.

At the same time, it is important to let young children express their grief. Parents can acknowledge children's feelings of sadness and anger while assuring them that they are in no way responsible for the loss of the loved one. Preschool children may find it particularly hard to accept the apparent senselessness of human death because they believe that important events serve some human purpose or have been caused by human intent.

One of the ways preschool children explore death is to include it in their pretend play. The same is true to a lesser extent of birth and growth. Parents can allow, even support, the children's efforts to create imaginary death scenes and funerals, or periods of imaginary pregnancy and delivery.

An enjoyable way to extend a child's conversation about the life process is to talk about the similarities and differences between people and animals. Many young children have a natural empathy for animals, and their respect for life is strengthened as they realize that animals, like people, are born, grow, and die. Within this common pattern, however, are a wealth of interesting and amusing differences. Some animals are hatched rather than born. Some are born with their eyes closed. Some are born without a father in the family. Each animal grows to a characteristic size. Some are small enough to live in little holes; others, having no home, keep wandering from spot to spot. All animals die, but their life expectancies are radically different. Some live peaceably, eating grass to survive. Some hunt other animals and kill them for food.

There is no particular set of comparisons between animals and humans that preschool children ought to discuss. It simply is fun to explore our kinship with other animals, to play with our observations, and to imagine a different sort of life. What would it be like to be hatched from an egg like a bird, to live in a nest until one day you started to fly? You could fly over fences, streets, rivers, go wherever you wanted. Of course, you'd have to sleep in a tree and eat worms. And you would have to make sure a cat didn't catch you and eat you for dinner.

PLAY IDEAS

Take your child to a farm and talk about baby animals. "See the cow. She's the mommy and those are her babies. They will look like their mommy when they grow up."

Read your child books about animals and their babies. Show your child a puppy and see if she can find the puppy's mommy.

When you are cooking dinner, talk about how chickens lay eggs, or how milk comes from a cow. Show your child a seed inside of a pumpkin and let him know that the seed turns into a pumpkin.

Give your child an opportunity to see and touch a newborn.

Helping Children Understand Growth

Put a measuring tape on the wall and mark it for your child. Does she recognize that growing taller and getting older go together?

Take out some of your preschooler's baby clothes. Talk about how small he was when he was little and how big he has grown.

Show your preschooler a family album. Can she find a picture of mommy and daddy when they were both babies?

Show your preschooler a butterfly. Show him how to hold his finger out and let the butterfly perch and then fly away.

Show your preschooler a dead ant. How does she know the ant is dead? What could have happened?

If your preschooler went to a funeral, let him replay the ceremony. Once he can pretend about death, coping with death is easier.

Read your child a book about death such as *Freddie the*

Leaf, by Leo Busgalia, or *Someone Special Died,* by Joan Single-ton. *Someone Special Died* is a picture book written to help young children understand and cope with the death of a loved one. These books will help him learn that death is a natural part of the life cycle.

SECTION II
ACTIVE PLAY

THE SWING

How do you like to go up in a swing,
Up in the air so blue?
Oh, I do think it the pleasantest thing
Ever a child can do!

Up in the air and over the wall,
Till I can see so wide,
Rivers and trees and cattle and all
Over the countryside—

Till I look down on the garden green,
Down on the roof so brown—
Up in the air I go flying again,
Up in the air and down!

—Robert Louis Stevenson

Active play, for most preschoolers, is a great way to have fun. Some preschoolers are daredevils, flying through the air on a swing, jumping down from high places, climbing up jungle gyms or into trees, or running down a hill at breakneck speed. Other children are more timid. They want to be pushed gently on a swing, jump down into the arms of a waiting parent, or play a relaxed and easy circle game like "Ring-a-Round the Rosy." But whether they are timid explorers or daring thrill seekers, preschool children strive to master physical skills. In this section we describe the motor skills that children are likely to practice, the active games they like to play, and the new sports they try to master.

All children tend to discover the same physical skills in the preschool years, although there are obvious differences in athletic interests and skill levels. Even more fascinating are differences in competitiveness, persistence, and personality. Some

57

children like to practice by themselves; others prefer to play with a peer or a grown-up. Some children are highly persistent, while others give up easily. Some children always have to win, while others want everyone to win. Some children are interested in learning a sport or game; others are more interested in running around, making up their own rules, or in acting out a pretend sports scenario.

In this section we look at how preschoolers practice physical skills and learn about the potentials of their own bodies. Three types of physical play are described: exercise play, game play, and trying out new sports.

CHAPTER 4

Exercise Play

~~~~~~~~~~~~~~~~~~~~~~~~~~~~~~~~~~~~~~~

EVERY TIME I CLIMB A TREE

Every time I climb a tree
Every time I climb a tree
Every time I climb a tree
I scrape a leg
Or skin a knee.
And every time I climb a tree
I find some ants
Or dodge a bee
And get the ants
All over me.

And every time I climb a tree
Where have you been?
They say to me.
But don't they know that I am free
Every time I climb a tree?
I like it best
To spot a nest
That has an egg
Or maybe three.

And then I skin
The other leg.
But every time I climb a tree
I see a lot of things to see

Swallows, roof tops, and TV
And all the fields and farms there be
Every time I climb a tree.

Though climbing may be good for ants
It isn't awfully good for pants.
But still it's pretty good for me
Every time I climb a tree.

—David McCord

"Watch me, watch me, I'm going to put my head all the way under . . . I'm doing a somersault . . . I can touch the bottom . . . watch me jump . . . watch me float on my back!"

As four-year-old Meling splashed around in the swimming pool, her demands for applause were nonstop. She had finally learned to put her head in the water and was close to learning to swim. Her mother, watching from the sidelines, was called upon to admire each new accomplishment. When her mother tried to convince her to come out of the pool, Meling, despite chattering teeth, pleaded for five more minutes.

The accomplishment of a new physical skill is very important to preschool children. Perhaps they remember back to toddlerhood, when each motor milestone was a cause for celebration. More likely, their delight with physical feats is associated with feelings of autonomy. The more things they can do with their bodies, the more independent they feel. Through play, they are discovering both the power and limitations of their own bodies.

In this chapter, we look at some of the motor skills preschool children practice, including walking and running, climbing up and jumping down, throwing and catching, and performing gymnastic feats.

WALKING AND RUNNING

"James is the fastest runner in the class, and me and Theresa are the second best runners," Nicholas reported to his parents. "You can't catch me," Carina challenged her mother as she ran across a field. "Watch how fast I can run," Fabian insisted as he walked cautiously across the lawn. Regardless of their skill level, running is a big accomplishment for the preschool child.

The first cluster of skills, walking and running, is usually well developed by the age of three. Clearly, however, children learn to run with greater proficiency and control during the preschool years. Their gait becomes much smoother, and they learn to start, stop, and turn quickly without falling down.

More dramatic is the development of specialized forms of walking and running. One of the first to appear is hopping. When asked to jump over a low obstacle, two-year-olds tend to give a little hop. Three-year-olds learn to hop vigorously. For a

while, in fact, they may hop continually, as if they were going to become rabbits. Human hopping is not worth much as a way of getting around, but it is immensely entertaining. As three-year-olds hop, they can hardly contain their giggling, and parents, caught up in the joke, find themselves hopping around, too. Sometime later, an even more peculiar behavior emerges: hopping on one foot. Again, the children go through a period of practice and experimentation, after which this unusual form of movement is channeled into games like hopscotch.

Hopping lives on in the form of the running broad jump. It takes several years of practice, however, to combine hopping and running skills. Standing at the edge of a puddle, the three-year-old is determined to jump over it. Then, at the last moment, her concentration falters and she stumbles right into the middle of the water. A year later, the child has a new idea. Now she will approach the puddle at a run, planning to sail across it with ease. Again, difficulty arises at a critical time, just when she is choosing which foot to take off with. Undecided, she sheepishly runs through the water on tiptoe. This jumping-the-puddle business is beginning to look like a Three Stooges routine. More time and more mishaps follow. Finally, the confident five-year-old approaches the puddle and properly jumps off with his leading foot. For a split second, everything looks right, but then, all too soon, the child lands with one foot partway across the puddle. It will take still more time to learn that the longest jumps are accomplished by landing with two feet.

Another kind of specialized running/ walking is even more silly and useless and therefore well suited to expressing exuberance and joy—skipping. Genuine skipping does not usually appear until children are near the end of the preschool period or even past it. Its predecessor, galloping, is popular among three—to five-year-olds. Galloping presumably makes a person feel more like a horse; anyway, it's what a horse would do if it had only two legs.

There is right-footed and left-footed galloping, and skipping is alternating between the two, first leading with the right foot, then with the left. The feeling of freedom that comes from galloping and skipping is positively therapeutic. Children cannot help but feel lighthearted when they discover that their feet will work in this crazy way.

Preschool children practice hopping and skipping just because they're fun to do, with no thought of additional benefits. Nevertheless, educators recognize a connection between mastering hopping and skipping and learning to read and write. The sense of balance, body awareness, left-right differentiation, and hand-eye coordination that children develop through hopping and skipping facilitates the acquisition of reading and writing skills.

JUMPING AND CLIMBING

Rosita, a young three-year-old, had just learned how to jump. When she visited a friend's house with her mother, she did not like the idea of going indoors. Her mother's friend had a large front porch with three steps leading up. While the friend stood outside greeting her mother, Rosita discovered that the front stairs were just right for practicing her newly acquired jumping skills. For the first five minutes Rosita climbed up and jumped down the lowest step. Encouraged by the applause of the adults, she got a little braver and jumped down all three steps, one step at a time. With each jump she turned around to make sure that her mother was watching. Finally, Rosita got brave enough to try a bigger jump. She stood on the second step with her feet together and jumped to the ground. "I'm a very good jumper," she informed the adults proudly. "You want to see me jump some more?"

Climbing up and jumping down form a natural routine. As we watch a toddler climbing on a stool and jumping down again, it is impossible to tell whether he or she is climbing for the joy of jumping or jumping for the joy of climbing. During the preschool years, children continue to practice and to elaborate their climbing and jumping skills. They master all the standard playground climbing structures and acquire an impressive repertoire of jumping skills.

The joy that children exhibit as they face a new challenge or master a new feat is justification enough for encouraging jumping and climbing. At the same time, it is important to recognize how much children learn about themselves and their environment as they test and develop these skills.

Although children do not have the words to express what they are learning, climbing and jumping provide object lessons in gravity. When children climb a pole, they feel themselves

resisting the downward pull of gravity. Jumping or sliding down gives them quite the opposite sensation. Gravity is working for them, and, for one brief second, they have the delicious sensation of weightlessness. Years hence, when a teacher talks about gravity, they will have had the experience-base to understand the concept.

In addition to helping children learn about gravity, jumping and climbing feats help children acquire a working knowledge of spatial relationships. When a child makes the decision whether or not to jump from a ledge or hand-walk across a bar, she is making some pretty sophisticated calculations.

THROWING AND CATCHING

"Catch, Daddy, catch, Daddy," Jordan shouted as he tossed a tennis ball across the living room. Fortunately, the tennis ball landed in the corner and nothing got broken. "Jordan," his father scolded, "How many times do I have to tell you? We do not throw balls in the living room."

Children learn to throw before they learn to catch. Their first experiments with throwing involve swinging their arms backwards and frontwards, opening their fist, and releasing the ball. When children first learn to throw it is not surprising that they cannot aim the ball. It is enough of a feat getting the ball to sail in the air without having to worry about where it will land.

Like Jordan, most preschoolers try to engage their parents in a game of catch. If a parent is assigned the role of catcher, he is expected to catch the ball wherever it is going. Catching and throwing are not easy skills to acquire. Catching requires following the trajectory of a ball, putting your hands in the right position, and closing your hands at just the right moment. Throwing involves thrusting the ball away from your body at a speed and in the direction that will make it possible to catch.

There are many different ways of developing the subskills of catching and throwing. Sitting on the floor and rolling a ball back and forth allows children to practice the turn-taking component. Hitting a balloon in the air gives children practice in predicting where and when the balloon comes down. Throwing a beach ball into a large wastebasket lets children practice aim. Throwing the beach ball back and forth with a parent gives children practice in catching. Although some children are less skilled in ball play than others, by the age of five most children are able to play a throwing and catching game with a large rubber ball.

GYMNASTIC FEATS

A final cluster of skills that preschool children work on are gymnastic feats. Here, the generic activity is tumbling. Once they have mastered a somersault, children experiment with different body positions and contortions. They work on backward somersaults and cartwheels. They learn how to hold their bodies stiff as they roll down a hill, or engage in a twirling game until they are too dizzy to stand up. Having mastered the ability to stay erect, children seem bent on discovering what the world would look like from another perspective.

Whether children are practicing running or gymnastic feats, an important aspect of the activity is attracting the atten-

tion of other children. In the pre-school years, sharing an exciting physical activity is a natural way to make friends. At four years old, Mason had developed a friendship with a hearing impaired peer. He described his friend to his mother: "Allen's ears don't work so good, but his arms and legs work fine."

SUGGESTIONS FOR PARENTS

The playground is the most common arena for parents and preschool children to enjoy physical play. Parents can add to the fun by sliding, swinging, or seesawing with their child. It is important, of course, to be alert to dangerous situations.

Here are some hazards:

- A merry-go-round that has a space between the turntable and the ground. Children can fall off and get an arm or foot caught underneath the spinning turntable.
- Swings, especially those with hard seats. Children can suffer head injuries when walking in front of or behind a moving swing.

- All climbing equipment that does not have a cushioned surface underneath, such as six inches of sand. There is no such thing as a climbing apparatus from which children can't fall.
- Horizontal bars, when an adult is not there to supervise. If a child tires halfway across, the only alternative is to drop down. Children can land on their elbows and receive serious injuries.
- Slides that do not have a landing with sides between the stairs and the slide. Children need a safe place to stand and wait their turn.

While it is important for parents to be aware of the kinds of equipment that can be dangerous, it is equally important not to be overprotective. Most preschool children have the capacity to judge for themselves how high they can climb and how far they can jump. When a piece of apparatus looks scary to them, they will make up excuses not to try it.

PLAY IDEAS

Play tug-of-war with your child using an old sheet.

Make an obstacle course in the yard using wastepaper baskets and cartons.

Make a pile of leaves and jump into it with your child.

Make a tunnel out of a carton and see if your child can roll a ball through the carton. This game, of course, is more fun if you stand on the other side and roll the ball back to your child.

Play follow the leader with your child.

On a breezy day, play bubbles with your child and challenge him to catch a bubble as it flies through the air.

Play kangaroo with your child, jumping or hopping around the yard.

Make a skipping rope out of running water from a hose. Hold the hose low to begin with and gradually make it higher.

Add to the fun of going on a walk by turning it into a scavenger hunt. Give your child a basket and see if he can collect five or six different objects: a big and small stone, a flower petal, an acorn or pine cone, a piece of paper, a maple leaf, and/or a pine needle. Keep a list of what you are looking for, and cross out each item as you find it.

Invite other children to the house and challenge the group to slither like snakes, walk on all fours, or tiptoe around like ballet dancers.

CHAPTER 5

Game Play

I will not play at tug o'war
I'd rather play at hug o'war
Where everyone hugs
Instead of tugs,
Where everyone giggles
And rolls on the rug,
Where everyone kisses,
And everyone grins,
And everyone cuddles,
And everyone wins.

—Shel Silverstein

Whether they are at home, at school, or at a party, children love to play active games. Some games are played with one friend. Others are played with a group of friends. "Ring-a-Round the Rosy" is one of the first games that children play. The rules are simple. Children spin around in a circle holding hands and chanting. When they reach the words "all fall down," everyone falls at the same time and everyone laughs hysterically.

In this chapter we describe three kinds of games: competitive games where one person is the winner; team games where one side or the other is the winner; and cooperative games where no one wins or loses. In the final section of the chapter we look at ways in which competitive games can be converted into cooperative games.

COMPETITIVE GAMES

Cassandra, who had just turned five, was excited about playing softball just like her two older sisters. When her parents let her join a T-Ball league, she was thrilled. Coached by her older sisters and her father, Cassandra learned how to hit a ball off a tee, catch a ball, and run around the bases. When Cassandra played in her first real game her sisters sat in the bleachers. First at bat, Cassandra delighted her sisters by hitting the ball off the tee and running around the bases. In the second half of the inning, when Cassandra's team were fielders, the coach put her on first base. The first child who was up at bat missed the ball several times and Cassandra decided to sit on the base. When the batter finally hit the ball, Cassandra sat beside the

base and did not pick up the ball. Her sisters were dismayed. "Why didn't you pick up the ball?" her sisters shouted as she walked off the field. "I couldn't pick it up," Cassandra explained. "I had to finish my sand castle." Children like Cassandra love the idea of playing a sport, but have no interest in winning or losing. The important part of playing T-Ball is wearing a uniform and running around the field.

Cassandra's lack of concern with winning and losing is not typical of all children. Most preschoolers enjoy playing competitive games such as "Mother May I," "Red Light, Green Light," "Simon Says," "Dodge Ball," and "Musical Chairs" precisely because they like to win. They love the fast pace of the games and are usually confident that they will be able to win. This confidence takes the sting out of losing. Unfortunately, children who are less agile, the ones who are eliminated from games very early and are relegated to the role of watcher, are often the children who could benefit most from participation in a competitive game.

Another downside to competitive games affects even the most agile child. Some children want to win a game so badly that they forget about playing fair and pout, shout, and withdraw from the game if someone else is the winner. Other children want to win so badly that they will find all kinds of devious ways to be the winner of the game.

Celia's mother, Muriel, a former preschool teacher, liked to invite the neighborhood children over to her house. On one rainy day she decided that the children would enjoy musical chairs.

Muriel: Everyone find a chair in the circle, and remember that you walk around the circle, and as soon as the music stops you have to sit in a chair. The children who find a chair get to stay in the circle. The last one in the circle is the winner.

Muriel began the first round of the game. Pedro, who was younger than the other children, was the first one to leave the circle. On the second round the chairs were farther apart and the children had to scramble to get in a chair. Celia stopped in front of each chair to make sure the music wasn't stopping. Her strategy worked, and she was still in the circle. Celia's mother removed another chair.

Muriel: Everybody ready—and remember, you have to keep walking until the music stops.

Muriel started the music and made sure not to stop it when one of the children was stalling in front of a chair. The three children left in the circle were poised to begin round three. When the music stopped Celia got to a chair about the same time as Donald, and gave him a little push so that she would get in the chair. "No fair," Donald shouted, "I got to the chair first and she pushed me off." Muriel took Donald by the hand and out of the circle.

Muriel: You're right, Donald. It is not fair to push. Anybody who pushes next time will be out of the game. You stand right beside me and let's be sure there is no pushing.

Celia and Horace were the last two in the circle. Muriel was careful to turn off the music when Celia was not near a chair. Horace, of course, was the winner. "He's a big cheater," Celia whined. "I don't want to play any more." Muriel expressed her concern to her husband when he came home that evening. "Celia is such a sweet child most of the time, but she is a terrible loser. She even finds ways to cheat so she can win the game."

Other mothers we spoke with expressed a similar concern. "My son loves to be the winner and is devastated when he doesn't win a game. He's so intent on being the winner that he really doesn't have fun playing the games."

Parents of "poor loser" children are likely to be concerned. Will their child will always be a poor sport? Are they are doing something wrong at home that makes winning so important?

Despite the problems they create for poor losers, competitive games have value. Knowing how to win without being boastful and to lose without getting upset is important throughout life and can begin in the preschool years. By playing competitive games with a humorous twist, parents can help children place less importance on winning. Katie, who was always the first to be sent to the middle of the circle in a game of "Duck, Duck, Goose" described the game to her grandmother. "First somebody chases somebody and if somebody catches you, you got to go in the mush pot. You get all mushed in the mushpot and it's fun." Katie's description of "Duck, Duck, Goose" is a good example of a competitive game with a silly twist that takes the sting out of losing.

Jordan, like Donald and Celia, would get upset when he wasn't the winner. Jordan's mother found that the best way to help Jordan was to tell him a story: "Alligator was very sad because he didn't have any friends. He was the fastest swimmer in the canal but one day he was tired and he lost the race. 'No fair,' he shouted to the other alligators. 'You all started out before I said one, two, three, go, and I'm not going to race with you any more.' He didn't understand why the other alligators wouldn't play with him anymore. Can you tell Alligator how to get his friends back?"

TEAM GAMES

Team games, in contrast to competitive games, give even the less skilled children an opportunity to be a winner. In order to be on the winning team, children must cooperate with and root for other team members. Another advantage of team games is that parents or teachers can select the members of the team so both sides have an opportunity to be winners. The problem with team games, however, is that children are likely to protest if unskilled or unpopular children are put on their team. They can also turn against anyone on their team who makes a mistake.

Miss Marilee: Okay, children, let's put all our toys away. It's time to go out on the playground.

Two children in chorus: Can we play "Red Rover, Red Rover," please, please?

Miss Marilee: That's a fine idea. I will choose the teams. I will tell you what team you are on. Peter—red, Davita—green, Chen—red, Allison—green, Arianna—red.

Peter: No way. I won't be on a team with Arianna.

Chen: Me either. She doesn't even know how to play.

Because team games with children under six are usually supervised by an adult, the adult has an opportunity to set up rules before the game that protect the less skilled child who is likely to be picked on by the group. The next time they played a team game, Miss Marilee announced the rules before the teams were selected. "Anyone who says, 'I don't want someone on my team' is not allowed to join the game. I hope that doesn't happen because I want everyone to have a chance to play."

COOPERATIVE GAMES

In contrast to competitive and team games, cooperative games don't have winners or losers. In a cooperative games everyone is included. Games where the children sit in a circle with an adult participating are the most popular of all cooperative games.

"Ring-a-Round the Rosy" is the prototype of circle games. As children begin the "Ring-a-Round" chant they walk around in a circle holding hands. When they chant the words "All fall down" the children stop circling, throw themselves on the

ground and laugh hilariously. Like "Ring-a-Round the Rosy" many of the circle games are traditional. Parents were taught the games by their own parents and in turn teach the games to their children.

Suzy: I learned a game in school today. It's called "Hokey Pokey." Want me to teach you?

Mom: Our family learned to sing that when I was little.

Suzy:Who teached you?

Mom: Grandma did.

Suzy:Who teached grandma?

Mom: Her mother, I guess.

Children love to play traditional circle games where the family can join in. At the same time, they like to learn new circle games that they can teach their parents.

Circle games, whether they are old or new, are appropriate for birthday parties. So often at birthday parties there is a group of children who know each other and play together, and a few children who are left on the sidelines. With cooperative circle games everybody can join the fun and no one is left out.

Kori's mother, Betty, was planning a party for Kori's fourth birthday. Recognizing that her daughter was timid and did not always join the play, Betty selected a variety of circle games that Kori, as well as her friends, would enjoy.

When the children arrived at the party, Betty let them play casually with some toys. Then, when everyone was there and had time for more organized play, she asked the children to sit on the floor in a circle.

Betty: I'm glad you're all in a circle because it's time to play "Sticky Popcorn."

Kori's friend: I never played "Sticky Popcorn."

Betty: Curl up in a ball and and pretend you are a kernel of popcorn. Oh, it's getting very hot in here! You are getting hotter and hotter. Oops, you are beginning to pop. [Kori, who had played the game before, jumped up from the floor, and all the children followed.] Oh, you are getting sticky. My goodness, you are beginning to stick together.

With great peals of laughter the children stood close to each other until they were all "stuck together" in the middle of the circle.

Betty: Back in the circle, everyone. It's time to play "Who stole the cookie?"

The children continued to play circle games until it was time for cake and ice cream. "That was the funnest party I ever had in my whole life," Kori told her mother after her friends went home.

Preschool children such as Kori and her friends love cooperative games. Having fun together, from the point of view of most preshool children, is more important than being a winner. Cooperative games give children an opportunity to laugh and be silly, to share the fun of chanting, to play with new or silly words, and to practice taking turns. A special benefit of cooperative games is that different cultures have their own versions of many of the games. As children play different versions of the same games, they are familiarized with their own and other cultures.

MAKING COMPETITIVE GAMES COOPERATIVE

Teachers who recognize the value of cooperative games find ways of changing the rules so that competitive games become cooperative.

Miss Janet: We're going to play musical chairs. When the music stops, everyone has to hurry up and scramble into a chair. Let's see if you can all be in your chairs before the music starts again.

Naturally, Miss Janet didn't turn the music back on until all the children were sitting in chairs.

Children: We did it! We want to play again!

On a different day, Miss Janet sent the children on a treasure hunt. "The goal of the hunt," she told the children, "is to find a rock with your name on it. When you find your own rock, you can help your friends find their rocks. I hope that everybody finds their rock before we have to go back into the classroom."

Another game that can be made cooperative by changing the rules is dodge ball. In cooperative dodge ball, the child who is hit by the ball becomes the first thrower in the next round. Every time there is a new thrower, one of the children from the circle goes back to the center. The game continues until everyone has had a turn being the thrower.

With some competitive games like "Hot Potato," thinking up a cooperative version of the game is more of a challenge. "Hot Potato" is usually a competitive game where children are out if they are holding the hot potato when the music stops. In a cooperative hot potato game, the children have to pass the potato around the circle three times before the music stops.

One of the delightful attributes of preschool children is that they are perfectly happy to join in a game where there are no winners or losers. With just a little ingenuity, parents and teachers can discover ways to make competitive games cooperative.

SUGGESTIONS FOR PARENTS

Preschool children need and love to play active games. Help your child learn several games that she can play with one or more friends. Introduce some games that are competitive, and some games that are cooperative. Be sure to include games that are spontaneous, where you and your child make up the rules.

PLAY IDEAS

Competitive Games

Think back to your childhood and try to remember some of the games you liked to play. Favorite traditional games where one child is the winner include "Hide and Seek," "Simon Says," and "Mother May I." Other choices include "Pin the Tail on the Donkey," tug-of-war, and tag.

Cooperative Games

Cooperative games are most fun when several children join in the play. Choose some games from the following selections:

Parachute

Children sit around a circle and hold onto a sheet with a bean bag on top. The purpose of the game is to see if the children can keep the bean bag on top of the sheet as they shake it up and down.

Balloon Play

Balloon play works well when there are only two to five players. In balloon play the children stand in a circle and the parent sings or plays a tape of favorite songs. Then he throws a balloon in the middle of the circle. The children try to keep batting the balloon in the air. If the balloon is still in the air when the song is over, then everyone is the winner.

Spontaneous Games

Some of the games that children enjoy most are made-up games that children play with their parents or other children. Gretchen and her family loved to play a game where someone hid the teddy bear and everyone had to look for it. Whoever found the teddy bear first could hide it on the next round of the game. Arran enjoyed playing a rolling game with his friends. He and his friends would roll down a hill in the park. Every time they succeeded in landing at the bottom at the same time, they laughed boisterously and ran back up the hill. Caroline called her favorite game "Animal Quackers." One member of the family pretended to be an animal with a distinctive way of moving. Caroline always went first. As she hopped like a kangaroo, waddled like a duck, or walked on all fours like a dog, the family lined up behind her and copied the way Caroline was walking. Then another member of the family was given a turn to lead the animal parade.

Circle Games

Children enjoy traditional games. In these games children stand in a circle, recite a chant, and make the motions suggested by the words. Here are a selection of games you might want to try out:

- "There's a Brown Girl in the Ring" is a favorite circle game from the Caribbean in which a child in the middle of the circle chooses a friend to join her and dance around the ring.

    There's a brown girl in the ring
    tra la la la la
    There's a brown girl in the ring
    tra la la la la

> *There's a brown girl in the ring*
> *tra la la la la*
> *For she likes sugar and I like plum.*
> *Then you skip across the ocean*
> *tra la la la la*
> *For she likes sugar and I like plum.*
> *Then you stand and face your partner*
> *tra la la la la*
> *For she likes sugar and I like plum.*
> *Then you show me your motion*
> *tra la la la la*
> *For she likes sugar and I like plum.*

- "Let's Get the Rhythm" is a circle game in which children perform a sequence of actions according to the words of the chant. Because the chant is rhythmic and repetitive, children can learn the words easily and join the chant.

> *Let's get the rhythm of the head (ding dong)*
> *Let's get the rhythm of the head (ding dong)*
> *Let's get the rhythm of the feet (stamp, stamp)*
> *Let's get the rhythm of the feet (stamp, stamp)*
> *Let's get the rhythm of the hands (clap, clap)*
> *Let's get the rhythm of the hands (clap, clap)*
> *Let's get the rhythm of the hot dog (swing hips in circle, hands*
>   *on hips)*
> *Let's get the rhythm of the hot dog (swing hips in circle, hands*
>   *on hips)*
> *Put it all together and what do you get?*
> *Ding-dong, stamp-stamp, clap-clap, hot dog.*
> *Put it all backward and what do you get?*
> *Hot dog, clap-clap, stamp-stamp, ding-dong.*

- "Waddily acha" is a hand clapping game with nonsense words:

Waddily acha, waddily acha, doodily do, doodily do
Waddily acha, waddily acha, doodily do, doodily do
It's a simple song, there's not much to it.
All you got to do is just doodily do it.
I like the rest, but the part I like best goes,
Doodily-doodily, doodily-doodily, doodily-doodily, doo-doo!

• "Punchinello" is a circle game where each child has a turn to get in the middle of the circle and perform an action that all the other children imitate.

What can you do, Punchinello, funny fellow?
What can you do, Punchinello, funny you? (Child does trick)
We can do it, too, Punchinello, funny fellow.
We can do it, too, Punchinello, funny you! (Others imitate child)

• "Little Sally Water" is a traditional circle game from the Caribbean. Children circle and pop up and down as they chant a short verse.

Little Sally Water
Sprinkle in a saucer.
Rise, Sally, rise, Sally, wipe off your eyes, Sally.
Turn to the east, Sally
Turn to the west, Sally
Turn to the very one you love the best.

• "Atwe Turi Entaama Ento (We are Little Lambs)" is a counting game from Uganda. Children stand in the circle and count together in Ugandan and English.

Amwe—one
Ebri—two

Ishatu—three
Ina—four
Itaano—five
Mukanga—six
Mushanju—seven
Mnana—eight
Mwenda—nine
Ikumu—ten

- "Beehive" is a finger play where children begin by cupping their hands to make a beehive and move their fingers one by one as the bees escape from the hive. It can be played as a circle or a partner game.

  Here is a beehive. (Hand cupped)
  Where are the bees?
  Hidden away where nobody sees.
  Soon they'll come creeping out of their hive
  1—2—3—4—5
  Bzzz, Bzzz, Bzzz. (Extend fingers one by one)

CHAPTER 6

Trying Out New Sports

〜〜〜〜〜〜〜〜〜〜〜〜〜〜〜〜〜

TAKE ME OUT TO THE BALLGAME

Take me out to the ball game,
Take me out with the crowd.
Buy me some peanuts and crackerjack
I don't care if I never get back.
Let me root, root, root for the home team.
If they don't win it's a shame.
For it's one, two, three strikes you're out
At the old ball game.

—Jack Norworth (lyricist)

Although preschool children spend much of their time practicing their physical skills, they are fully aware that older children and grown-ups participate in a variety of different kinds of athletic activities. Grown-up sports often require special equipment and fancy uniforms. Naturally, preschool children are attracted to these activities. In this chapter we provide samples of group sports and individual sports that children can try out.

When preschool children play at sports, their performance bears a strong resemblance to pretending. A game of tennis between two young preschoolers may be little more than randomly hitting a tennis ball, accompanied by phrases they've heard: "Net ball," "Your serve," "Love, one, two, seven." Older preschool children can temporarily organize teams. In the following example, most of the five-year-olds in a preschool class were involved in an impromptu basketball game. The result is impressive but not much like a real game of basketball.

Davita, as self-appointed coach and referee, started the game by selecting the teams, Singva and Brian against Erik and Jerome. There was no coordination between team members. Whoever had the ball ran in circles around a box (which served as the basketball hoop), while the other three alternated between yelling for the ball and trying to block the path to the goal. Occasionally, someone got close enough to the box to toss or drop in the ball. Davita, as score keeper, sat inside an orange plastic tire. Davita shouted out the score periodically. The game stopped several times because of disputes, and the boys went to Davita for arbitration. For example, Singva got a rebound, which Erik considered unfair. Davita made the two boys shake hands and warned Singva, "You better not do that again."

Some of the watchers began to chant encouragement. Davita gathered them into a huddle and instructed them to cheer for Singva. Then she rushed back to the coach's circle in

order to keep the game going. Sensing that fate was on his side, Singva yelled several times, "We win." Apparently he had guessed right. Davita signaled the end of the game by leading away Erik, one of Singva's opponents. She put her arm around him and said in her artificial adult voice, "You're a good loser." Then she found Jerome, Erik's supposed partner, and consoled him in the same way.

GROUP SPORTS

Few preschool children are prepared for the complexities of participating in organized sports. However, all preschoolers can benefit from an introduction to the simpler skills of various athletic activities.

Of the team sports, the easiest one for preschool children to play is soccer. The children can practice dribbling the ball and kicking it into a homemade goal. A parent and child can play soccer by simply racing to the ball and kicking it in differ-

ent directions around the yard. Basketball, if it involves a lightweight ball and lowered standards, is also suitable for preschool children. They can dribble, shoot, and pass. The rules of baseball are considerably more complicated, and it is virtually impossible for preschool children to hit the ball within the limit of three strikes. If you use a tee to hold the ball, and if you're willing to explain the rules countless times, a version of baseball may emerge. Football, with preschool children, is strictly a pretend activity, a kind of tag in which one person carries a football.

Baseball and football, if children are interested, provide a special opportunity to develop throwing and catching skills. When children play a throw and catch game with each other the game is short-lived because it is too discouraging to keep chasing the ball. Even with parents who throw the ball carefully and help retrieve errant balls, children want to go on to something else after five or ten minutes. Playing catch with a balloon or a Frisbee, while not part of an "adult" sport, may prove to be more fun.

INDIVIDUAL SPORTS

At three years old, riding a tricycle was a difficult challenge for Chen. He got the idea of pushing down a peddle, but couldn't figure out how to make the peddles go around. Finally, after his father pushed him around the block several times, Chen recognized that each leg had to have a turn pushing down while the opposite leg went up. By four years old, Chen was an excellent rider. He and his friend Peter chased each other around the path, bumping their tricycles on purpose and laughing hysterically. Pretty soon they challenged each other to do tricks: riding down a hill, racing around in tight circles, and catapulting their tricycles down a step with breakneck speed.

Whether we are watching preschool children racing around on a tricycle, swinging golf clubs with all their might, or zooming down a slide, it is clear that more is involved in such activities than skill development. The children are experiencing powerful emotions. They have discovered the attractions of force and speed. "Watch me," shouted Amelia, as she pumped her swing higher and higher. "I'm a bird, I'm an airplane, I'm Superwoman!"

Although preschool children are unlikely to learn a grown-up game, they do enjoy individual sports. Katie, at four years old, learned to ski in one easy lesson and was soon out skiing with her parents. When her parents introduced her to riding, however, Katie took one look at the horse and decided her tummy was hurting. With Danny it was quite the opposite. On his very first pony ride he trotted around the ring and announced that he was a cowboy. When his parents brought him to a ski slope he explained that he would rather go swimming.

Most children by the age of three, when given the opportunity, are ready to learn how to swim. Although some parents enroll their children in a swimming course, children are likely to be more confident when a parent is their first teacher. After all, the hardest part of learning to swim is putting your head in the water. With a parent there to catch you it isn't quite as scary.

EXPERIMENTING WITH FORCE AND SPEED

The athletic feats of preschoolers, whether extensions of old skills or first efforts to play sports, give children the opportunity to learn about the capabilities of their bodies. They learn that people can climb, jump, and run in different ways. On a more subtle level, they learn to recognize and experiment with force and speed. These two ideas seem to be particularly intriguing to preschool children. They want to be as strong as possible and go as fast as they dare.

Force is involved in pushing a tire swing, kicking a ball, throwing a Frisbee, and many other physical activities. Sports equipment can dramatically magnify a child's perception of strength. Children love using equipment designed for hitting balls: golf clubs, bats, croquet mallets, tennis racquets, ping-pong paddles, and so on.

Speed is also an important concept in most of these physical activities. In fact, children find that moderate increases in speed enhance most activities. Most preschoolers are not ready for the world of high speed, but they actively expand their limits. They try taller slides and learn how to gain speed by raising their legs. Or they may try out a variety of sliding techniques: sliding on their stomachs, sliding head first, even running down the slide. Such experiments seem to intensify the perception of speed. The trip down seems faster as it becomes more novel.

The physical skills preschool children develop play an important role in their relationships with other people. Parents take pride in the physical accomplishments of their children. The peer group admires physical prowess. In this chapter, however, we have described the development of physical skills as a means of self-discovery for preschool children. Physical play is an end in itself. During the preschool years, children discover that their bodies have surprising physical possibilities and they begin to appreciate the potential excitement of athletic force and speed.

SUGGESTIONS FOR PARENTS

Parents play an important role in sparking their child's interest in group sports. Try to engage your child in a sport that you play or that she has watched. Whether it is basketball, soccer, baseball, or hockey, the sport will have no appeal to a child if they haven't watched it being played.

Baseball

First, let your child watch neighborhood children playing softball. Buy your child a plastic bat and a whiffle ball. String the ball from a tree branch and let your child hit the whiffle ball with the bat. Be sure to let your child wear a baseball cap. For most children, the important part of playing baseball is wearing the appropriate attire.

Basketball

A large wastebasket makes a fine hoop. Buy a toy basketball and show your child how to bounce the ball and then toss it into the basket. Basketball is often much more fun when another child joins the game.

Hockey

Whether you live in a hot or cold climate, your child will enjoy a modified game of hockey. Buy a toy hockey stick and puck, or use child size brooms and tennis balls. In the beginning, you should play hockey with your child. Bringing in a friend can turn too easily into a hitting game.

Swimming

- Encourage your child to put his head under water but do not force the issue (practicing in the bathtub may be less frightening to your child than in the pool).
- Let your child jump and play in the water before you begin your lesson.
- For the first lesson, pass your child back and forth between yourself and a partner.
- Move farther apart from your partner as your child is ready to move into the water alone.
- Do not work on strokes until your child can stay afloat dog-paddle style.
- Invite children who swim just a little better than your child as models.

PLAY IDEAS

You and your child can take turns pretending to play a sport. See if your child can recognize what sport you are playing.

With your child, watch an individual sport such as golf on television. "Talk" to the player as he engages in the sport. "Tiger, keep your head down. Hit the ball hard." Give your child a turn talking to the player.

Watch a team sport such as a Major League baseball game together with your child. Look through the paper the next day and see if you can find a picture of an important play. Ask your child to talk about the picture.

Collect baseball or football cards with your child. See if she can remember a name of a player that she has seen in a baseball game on television.

THE SCIENTIST AT WORK

MIRACLES

Why, who makes much of a miracle?
As to me, I know of nothing but miracles.
To me every hour of the light and dark is a miracle.
Every cubic inch of space is a miracle.
Every area of the surface of the earth is spread with
the same substance.
Every foot of the interior swarms with the same sub-
stance.
To me, the sea is a continual miracle.
The fishes that swim, the rocks,
The motion of the waves, the ships with men in them.
What stranger miracles are there?

—Walt Whitman

Jerome is playing in his backyard. First he digs a trench in a mud pile behind his house and watches rivulets of water wind around his barricades. Then he fills his sand pail with mud and dumps it onto the driveway. After several pails of mud have been dumped, he hunts around for twigs that he plants on top of the pile. "That is a very good bear trap," he announces to no one in particular.

Children are endowed with all the critical qualities of a true scientist: a passion for experimentation, a kinship with nature, an inborn sense of wonder, and an incessant need to know. Although from time to time we may end up having to admire a squirming earthworm or tolerate a messy kitchen, the scientific spirit in young children must be preserved and nurtured.

This section includes three chapters. Chapter 7, "Investigations," describes the discoveries children make as they investigate their world; Chapter 8, "Transformations," describes ways in which children experiment with making changes; and Chapter 9, "The Naturalist," describes children's budding interest in plants and animals.

Investigations

AT THE SEASIDE

When I was down beside the sea
A wooden spade they gave to me
To dig the sandy shore.
My holes were empty like a cup
In every hole the sea came up.
Till it could come no more.

—Robert Louis Stevenson

Preschool children are curious. They want to know what mud feels like when you run it through your fingers, and what happens to ice if you leave it out in the sun. They are especially interested in plants and animals. How does a spider spin a web, and what makes a plant grow bigger? In this chapter we look at some of the ways in which preschool children carry out their scientific investigations.

Children first learn about their world through their senses: feeling, smelling, tasting, listening, and watching. As children continue their investigations, they learn about the properties of different substances. They discover that two substances can be alike in some ways and different in others, and they become adept at recognizing different substances which they have already encountered. The more aware children become of the

properties of the different substances, the more likely they are to develop strong opinions about what they like and what they don't like. Brenan told his mother that he hated broccoli and he would not eat his dinner. "Well, then, leave the broccoli on the plate and eat the rest of your dinner," his mother suggested. "No way," Brenan insisted, "you made my whole dinner smell like broccoli."

SENSORY PLAY

Carlos and his friend Katerina were playing on the beach.

Carlos: Let's bury our toes in the sand.
Katerina: Okay. No, I have a better idea. I'll bury your toes and you bury mine.
Carlos: Stop wiggling your toes. I can't get them buried. Oh look, I made a hole in the sand.
Katerina: I made a bigger hole.
Carlos: My hole is even gianter.
Katerina: There's a giant in my hole.

Both children dig up Katerina's hole.

Carlos: No, two giants. Hear 'em, they're making scary noises.
Katerina (in a loud low "giant" voice): Fee-fi-fo-fum—me needs a castle.

Carlos and Katerina continue to talk for the giants as they work at building a sand castle.

Like Carlos and Katerina, most preschoolers learn from the sensory play in which they love to engage. Playing in the sand at the beach provides an opportunity for casual conversation as children discover the different ways they can play with sand. Sometimes sensory play is an occasion for systematic scientific investigation. Children go beyond the sensual pleasure of handling a substance and focus their attention on how the substance can be changed.

Gregory: Look at that. All the water from my bottle fit into the blue pail.
Luisa: Yeah, that's cool. Try pouring it back again.
Gregory: Okay. Hold the bottle. Oops! Don't let it spill.

As Gregory and Luisa continue with their water play, they discover that they can keep changing containers and still have

the same amount of water. This characteristic of water is obvious to adults, but for a preschool child it is an important discovery.

While water play leads to spontaneous experiments with liquids and volume, sand play allows children to create solid forms with their hands. Given a pile of wet sand, children almost instinctively shape it into a castle or make a row of sand cakes. Although they may not describe their discoveries in words, children are learning that the shape of a substance can be changed without otherwise changing the substance.

SIMILARITIES AND DIFFERENCES

As children continue to play with different kinds of materials, they make an equally important discovery: things can be alike in some ways but quite different in other ways.

Peter loved to play with shells. As he put his shells into different piles, Peter picked up each shell and talked to it. "Your name is Conch. You have to go in the conch pile. I have lots of conches. Oops, sorry, conch. You have a pink underneath. You have to go in my pile of pink shells." As Peter continued his soliloquy, his father, who was watching, grew more and more impressed by his son. Even if Peter sometimes changed the basis of his sort, he was able to name the shells and recognize subtle differences.

Children, like Peter, have an amazing capacity to recognize things that are alike in some ways and different in others. They can sort things into several categories, and can recognize an object by its sound, feel, taste, or smell.

Fabian was visiting his aunt. When he went into the kitchen he was fascinated by all the gadgets that made noises. The bread maker rang when the bread rose, the oven beeped when the turkey was ready, the dryer buzzed when the clothes were dry, and the roasting oven whistled when the potatoes were brown. Fabian and his aunt were playing checkers in the family room when they heard something beep. "Time to get the towels out of the dryer," Fabian announced. "How do you know it's the dryer?" his aunt asked. "Because it sounds like a dryer," Fabian answered matter-of-factly. Fabian was just as accurate at identifying smells. "That man smells like smoke," he remarked when a delivery man came to the door.

Children are not only adept at recognizing minor distinctions, they can also take in information from one sense and describe its effect on a different sense. Children learn how something tastes by the way it looks or smells, and how something feels by the way it looks.

Jordana: I see a birdie.
Mother: Where do you see one?
Jordana: In that tree over there.
Mother: You mean you hear a bird.
Jordana: I see a bird. He's yellow and he's singing from that tree.

Jordana's mother was right. There was no way Jordana could see a bird on the top of the tree from where she was standing. Still, from Jordana's point of view, she was being perfectly accurate. Earlier in the day a bird had been standing on a branch in the tree trilling nonstop. Jordana watched the bird for a long time, and told her mother how pretty it looked. "I can hear the bird, but I can't see it," her mother said. "I don't see it for real either," Jordana admitted, "but I see what he looked like when we saw him by the lake. Remember how he was making that twill sound?"

Kori had no trouble knowing how something felt by the way it looked. Shopping for clothes for Kori was always a chore.

Kori: I don't want that dress. It has a big tag and it itches.
Kori's mother: We could always take the tag off.
Kori: No, it still itches in the place you took the tag off.

LIKES AND DISLIKES

Much to the consternation of their parents, preschool children have decided likes and dislikes. When Carlos and his parents were eating dinner at a guest's house, Carlos was served a small portion of cauliflower. Although his mother had told him to just try it and see if he liked it, Carlos took one look at the cauliflower and announced in a loud voice, "I hate cauliflower, it tastes yucky." Oliver's mother reported a similar incident when they were visiting a neighbor who invited them to stay for dinner. "I don't want cabbage," he whispered to his mother. "How do you know you don't want cabbage?" his mother whispered back. "You haven't ever tasted it." "Well I'm not going to taste it," Oliver replied in a too loud voice. "It smells awful."

Children's tactless expression of their likes and dislikes should not be interpreted as rudeness. Three- to five-year-olds have an uncanny ability to detect minute variations in the way things feel, sound, taste, smell, and look.

SUGGESTIONS FOR PARENTS

With very young children, sensory play is associated with making a mess. Two-year-olds pour the orange juice on the floor, finger paint with chocolate pudding, and splash the bath water until the whole bathroom is wet. Although preschool children are supposed to know better, they too can get carried away by the fun of making a mess. Parents are rightfully disturbed by messiness when it occurs in the wrong place. Organizing sensory play in an appropriate place—outside, perhaps, or in the bathtub, or even in the kitchen—will enable children to enjoy the benefits of making a mess without upsetting the house.

Out-of-doors is the ideal place for messy play, when the weather permits it. Mud and water are likely to be available,

and even if the play gets exuberant, nothing can be damaged. To encourage scientific experimentation and add to the fun of mud play, supply your child with a variety of shovels, wooden spoons, and empty plastic containers of different shapes and sizes. If you are concerned about your child digging up the garden, fill a sandbox or tub with earth and let your child add water. Children often get interested in changing the consistency of the mud by adding different amounts of water.

Finger painting is another sensory activity that works well outside. To avoid torn and wasted paper, let your child finger paint on plastic or vinyl place mats or on an old plastic tablecloth. Make sure that there is a

source of water around (a hose is ideal) that can wash away a finished picture. Let the children wash away their own pictures when they are ready. You may also want to give your child tools such as cotton swabs, plastic knives, or jar lids that can be used to make designs in the finger painting.

The bathtub is an ideal spot for sensory play with water, shaving cream, ice cubes, and soap bubbles. Again, the play can be extended by simple props: plastic glasses, strainers, sifters, mixing spoons, funnels, and containers of different shapes and sizes. Inevitably, the play will turn to cooking and parents might be asked to taste a soapy ice cream soda. Interestingly, some parents object to this type of play because they think of it as regressive. Put this fear to rest. Sensory play not only leads to scientific discovery, it is also an end in itself. Because sensory play with liquid or semiliquid materials is relaxing and unde-

manding, it has a calming effect on children who tend to get overactive.

Moving from the bathroom to the kitchen provides opportunities for real as well as pretend cooking. With supervision, preschool children can learn to crack an egg, whip potatoes, mix Jell-O, or prepare their own sandwiches. They also enjoy making their own concoctions: mixing juice and milk, adding seasoning to soup, decorating brownies or pancakes, and inventing new sandwiches, salads, or casseroles. These cooking activities do not always produce an edible product, but they do give children firsthand experience with creating transformations.

PLAY IDEAS

"Seeing" Games

Play games with your child that encourage matching and attention to detail. Take your child on a walk around the block. Gather leaves from several different trees. Talk about ways in which the leaves from different trees are different from each other. Make a scrapbook with your child. Glue a leaf on a page of the scrapbook and let your child find a "twin" to put on the opposite page. Continue the game so long as your child enjoys it.

Find two decks of playing cards. Choose eight matching cards from the deck. Put one set in a row in front of your child and one set in a row in front of you. Begin by asking your child to take out one card and put it in the middle; find your matching card and put it on top. As you find a matching card, talk about what you are doing. "Your card has two hearts, and I am finding my card with two hearts and putting it on top of your card. Now it's my turn to put down a card. Can you find a card that looks just like mine?" Make the game easier by using fewer cards. Make the game more challenging by adding more cards. Play the same kind of matching game with strips of colored construction paper. If your child enjoys the game, help her make a paper chain with alternating colors. If she's interested, you can progress to more complex patterns.

"Listening" Games

Create a sound matching game for your child. Find eight empty film cans. Put in small items such as pennies, large paper clips, screws, and sand in the cans, making two cans of each

kind. Let your child shake each can and find the cans with the same sound. Make a game out of it by taking your turn shaking the cans. Once in a while make an intentional mistake, open the two cans and say, "Oops, I guessed wrong." Children need to know that making a mistake is fine.

Put out a wooden bowl, a pan, a pan cover, and a box. Strike one of the items with a wooden spoon. Ask your child to close his eyes. Give him the spoon and see if he can make the same sound you did. Give your child a turn to be the first one to strike the "drum."

"Smelling" Games

Take cotton squares and put different scents on each pair of squares: for example, perfume, toothpaste, cinnamon, and peppermint. See if your child can find the squares that smell alike.

"Feeling" Games

Put some miniature animals in a paper bag. Put a line of matching animals in front of your child. Ask your child to reach in the bag and find one of the animals, guessing what it is before he takes it out of the bag. When he finishes the task, say, "Great, now each animal has a friend." If he makes a mistake say, "Oops, you need to try again."

The preschool period is an important time to help your child refine his sensory perceptions. Sensory input—sounds, tastes, smells, textures, and sights—are the bases for discoveries your child makes about his world. Skills that are not developed in the early years are more difficult to master in later years. A preschool child who is exposed to a second language will understand and speak that language in a very short time without being taught. The older the child, the more difficult it becomes.

Take advantage of your child's exciting capabilities. Give him real world experiences by going to a petting zoo, watching an earthworm wriggle through the grass, tasting different foods, and feeling soft things, rough things, slippery things, and prickly things.

CHAPTER 8

Transformations

~~~~~~~~~~~~~~~~~~~~~~~~~~~~~~~~~~~~~

HUMPTY-DUMPTY

Humpty-Dumpty sat on a wall.
Humpty-Dumpty had a great fall.
All the king's horses,
And all the king's men,
Couldn't put Humpty together again.

Hans was sitting in the bathtub playing with an empty shampoo bottle and a cube with holes on the bottom. When his mother suggested that it was time to get out, Hans explained that he was too busy. As his mother watched, Hans

"sifted" cold water through the cube into the shampoo bottle. Next he turned on the hot water tap and "sifted" in some hot water. With his thumb covering the opening, he turned the shampoo bottle upside down and gave it a good shake. "I'm making a weather tester," he announced proudly.

Hans's mother told us, "Although I knew perfectly well that Hans was just playing in the bathtub, I had to give him credit. Nobody except Hans could come up with an idea like that."

It was obvious to Hans's mother that Hans was having fun with the shampoo bottle and she let Hans play in the bath for another ten minutes. "Our son is quite a kid," she told her husband. "After all, how could I disturb a budding scientist in the middle of an experiment?"

Unquestionably, Hans's weather tester explanation was an afterthought. Four-year-olds are also quite clever at finding ways to explain away deviations from their original intentions.

Rosita and Peter were playing with Play-Doh.®

Peter: I got the clay first. I'm making a Humpty-Dumpty. (Peter took a large hand-ful of Play-Doh and made a sort of egg-shaped ball.)
Rosita: Give me clay. It's my turn.
Peter: It's not your turn. I gotta make more Humpty-Dumpties.
Rosita: It is so my turn.
Peter: Not! (He put the first Humpty-Dumpty on the table and began to make an-other one.)
Rosita (knocking at the Play-Doh table with one quick swipe): Had a big fall.
Peter: My turn. Humpty-Dumpty fell off.

Peter and Rosita continued the game, giggling, until the last piece of clay was on the floor. Rosita looked down at the squashed Humpty-Dumpty. "Look at my tortilla," she shouted, as she picked up some flattened clay from the floor.

Children like Peter and Rosita love pulling things into

pieces, or breaking things apart, and then, quite by accident, creating something else.

Playing with clay or mud allows children to control transformations. Clay can be compressed into a ball, then rolled out, then squeezed once more into a ball. Or perhaps it is transformed from a ball to a hot-dog shape and then back again. A variation on this theme is to stamp a design into the mud or clay. The child can then "erase" the design by rubbing it with his finger or a roller.

In this chapter we look at two aspects of making a transformation: taking things apart and putting things back together.

TAKING THINGS APART

Transformations can also be explored through solid objects that come apart and fit back together. As every parent knows, children are capable of taking objects apart long before their third birthdays. Naturally they get better at it between the ages of three and five. A dramatic new development is the ability to use tools for this purpose.

A pair of scissors is unquestionably a favorite tool for taking things apart. When a child first attempts to use scissors, the goal is simply to open and close the blades. Holding the scissors at right angles to the paper, which requires both skill and insight, can take time and the child may need help to accomplish it. The next major breakthrough is learning how to continue the opening/closing motion until the paper is cut in half. The final step in cutting involves controlling the direction of the scissors. Once this is accomplished, the child will be able to follow an outline with the scissors and cut out shapes without help.

Knives, like scissors, have a double value for children. Using a knife is both a grown-up skill and a means of taking

things apart. Since knives are more dangerous than scissors, parents are rightfully concerned about their use. Interestingly, parents who do allow their children to use knives report very few accidents. Children, for the most part, have a built-in fear of danger, especially when that danger is in their own hands.

Veronica's mother always involved her children in cooking. She had three sections in her cutlery drawer, one section for "little-girl" knives, one section for "big-girl" knives, and one section for "adult-only" knives. The highlight of turning four for Veronica was graduating to the "big-girl" section of the drawer. "Now I can use the knife with a 'stir-ated' edge," she proudly told her daddy.

Other tools for taking things apart are often too difficult for preschool children to use successfully. A saw, for example, requires so much force that a child grows weary before the board is cut in two. A screwdriver slips when the child tries to remove screws but is useful for taking things apart by prying.

PUTTING THINGS BACK TOGETHER

Preschool children who learn to take things apart will eventually want to fit the pieces together again. (In fact, a child using scissors may want to fit the paper together before he or she has fully taken it apart.) The ability of tools like glue, tape, and staples to combine pieces of paper is engrossing. Gregory, who had a particular love for saving odd bits and pieces of things, would spend a lot of time taping these treasures together. One day he taped together a bracelet, some bits of string, several baseball cards, and a gum wrapper. "Look, Ma," he said proudly, holding up his creation. "I made a walkie-talkie."

During the preschool period, children become noticeably better at fitting two objects together. They like to dress and undress dolls, build with Legos,® and make paper-clip chains. They recognize how one object must be turned so that it will fit precisely with the second object, and they realize the angle with which force must be applied to join the two objects. Quite frequently, however, they focus so intently on the process of fitting that they overlook the larger context. A child will work and work to get two puzzle pieces together, not noticing that they are different colors or that one is an edge piece and the other belongs in the middle of the puzzle.

A jigsaw puzzle looks like a simple "fit-together" kind of problem when it really involves much more. In order to put a puzzle together, it is necessary to consider the relationship between the parts and the whole. Preschool children have difficulty thinking in this way, although there are signs they are making progress. With blocks or Legos younger children simply try to make as large a structure as possible. Later, they are able to take into account part/whole relationships so they can construct particular forms. Similarly, younger preschool children focus on filling up every hole when playing with a pegboard, while older children fill up the board with intentional

designs. This progress in creating structures or designs is generally quite slow. The ability to coordinate fitting-together skills with larger plans remains limited and rigid. A child who has learned to make a Lego car or a Lite-Brite® design tends to follow the same plan every time, according to a memorized formula.

The most popular "put together" activity is cooking. Preschool children love making "concoctions" in the kitchen, particularly when no adult is telling them what to do.

Brenan had his first glass of eggnog at a friend's house. It was "awesome," he told his sister when he got home. The next

morning Brenan poured his orange juice into his milk. "What on earth are you doing?" his mother asked. "Making a glass of eggnog," Brenan answered matter-of-factly.

While Brenan's eggnog experiment could be classified as a transformation, many "put together" activities such as pasting, stapling, or making a pile of magnets do not involve a change in the final product. The fun in put together activities is not in making something different, but in making two substances stick together.

SUGGESTIONS FOR PARENTS

While sensory motor play with different kinds of semi-liquids is fun and relaxing, putting together objects is an activity that offers a greater challenge and requires more concentration. One of the problems that children face is that the pieces of a fit-together toy are easy to lose or mix-up. You can help your child keep the pieces of a toy sorted by providing different colored boxes or containers for the different kinds of toys.

Decide on one or two types of put-together toys, and add to that collection rather than getting your child a set of each new toy that goes on the market. In selecting a put-together toy, take into account your child's limited muscle coordination. No matter how good your child is with constructing, toys that are too difficult to join together are bound to cause frustration.

The most satisfactory fit-together toys are ones that allow children to create a variety of products. Children start with the initial challenge of fitting the pieces together and progress at their own rate toward planned construction. A trial-and-error strategy does not necessarily lead to frustration.

Puzzles, on the other hand, have a single solution. Some children seem to have a special talent for puzzles and can find the solution with no input from an adult. More frequently, children need help. One way to help a child is to do the puzzle yourself, talking out loud about what you are doing. "Yes, this is the leg of a horse. It must go on the bottom of the puzzle. The horse is standing up. His tail goes over here. Oops, it doesn't fit. Should I turn it the other way?"

A second strategy is to help your child plan the puzzle by putting like pieces together. You could help your child make a pile of all the yellow pieces or all the pieces that are a part of a bunch of balloons. For more complicated jigsaw puzzles, you can help your child find the edges. If your child continues to have problems, you may want to do most of the puzzle yourself, letting him or her have the fun of putting in the last pieces.

Even when a child knows how to put a puzzle together, a puzzle might end up in pieces. After all, it's much easier and often more fun to take puzzles apart than to put them back together again.

If a child has completed the same puzzle several times and wants to move on to another activity, it is much more logical and certainly easier, from the child's viewpoint, to end the activity with the puzzle dumped on the floor.

PLAY IDEAS

Give your child a jar of paste, a large sheet of paper, and many paper scraps. Encourage him to use the paste to stick the scraps onto the sheet of paper.

Give your child scraps of styrofoam, a small hammer, and nails or golf tees. See if he can piece the styrofoam together using the nails or golf tees.

Give your child a hole puncher, two paper plates, and some yarn. See if your child can attach the plates together by threading the yarn through the holes she makes with the hole puncher.

Cook some spaghetti and leave it in the refrigerator for a few days. The spaghetti will now stick to paper. Give your child a paper plate and the spaghetti. Let him make a spaghetti picture.

Give your child a box with a lid and some string. See if she enjoys wrapping the string around the box to keep the lid on.

Tear a piece of paper in half. Give your child a roll of tape so that he can put the two halves back together.

CHAPTER 9

The Naturalist

NOISE, BY POOH

Oh, the honey-bees are gumming
On their little wings, and humming
That the summer, which is coming,
Will be fun.

And the cows are almost cooing,
And the turtle-doves are mooing,
Which is why a Pooh is poohing
In the sun.

For the spring is really springing;
You can see the skylark singing,
And the blue-bells, which are ringing,
Can be heard.

And the cuckoo isn't cooing,
But he's cucking and he's ooing,
And a Pooh is simply poohing
Like a bird.

—A. A. Milne

We have talked so far, about ways in which children investigate their physical world: mixing and pouring, poking and pounding, pulling apart and sticking back together. In contrast to the child as a physical scientist, the child as a natural scientist is much more of an observer. He watches motionless as a spider spins a web or a bee sucks nectar from a flower. Eventually these observations lead to questions: What does the animal eat? Where does he live? Does he have sisters and brothers? As the child becomes more familiar with an animal, he searches for ways of making closer contact. He wants to bring the animal into his home where he can watch it more closely and take care of it.

ANIMALS

Household pets provide children with an opportunity to make friends with an animal. The type of companionship a pet friend offers to a young child is determined for the most part by the kind of pet it is. Kittens are cuddly and playful but not very good as protectors. Rabbits are fun to feed and look at, but they may not want to be cuddled. Small dogs are good for chase games and ball play, but big dogs are better as protectors.

When we talked to parents of preschool children about their family pets, one point was made consistently. No matter how many pets there were in the house, the family dog had a special status. From the point of view of the preschool child, the dog was a family member. "You don't got to be scared of him," Brenan explained to a visitor who was looking timidly at their Great Dane. "He's a people dog."

Children who think about dogs as family members are likely to believe that dogs share human emotions. When Kenneth was visiting his cousins, he was introduced to their dachshund. Kenneth paid no attention to the dog until the family was on their way out for dinner. When he realized the dog was being left behind, his face registered shock. "But who is going to stay with Kim?" he asked plaintively. "Kim is only a baby."

While dogs and cats are the favorite pets of preschool children, close attachments to other kinds of animals are not unusual. Hans, who had a special fondness for insects and crawling things, developed a strong attachment to his pet snail, Snorpy. One day, his mother found Snorpy dead on the bottom of the aquarium. She decided to save the shell for Hans as a way for him to remember his friend. With a look of horror, Hans took the shell from his mother and ran out of the room. A few minutes later, Hans came back to the room with quivering lips and teary eyes. "Mommy," he pleaded in a pathetic voice. "I just gave Snorpy a kiss because I miss him. Can we go to the lake and get another snail?"

Like Hans, many preschool children develop tender feelings for animals even when they do not have the status of family pets. Kenneth and his mother had visited a relative at the hospital and were waiting outside on the steps. While his mother was talking to a friend, Kenneth slipped from her side. A few seconds later, he returned carrying a dead blackbird. Caught by surprise, his mother told him to drop the bird immediately. "But, Mommy," Kenneth pleaded with tears in his eyes, "can't I take it to Emergency?"

Although most parents are pleased with their children's attachment to pets, the question of responsibility often comes up as a problem. Promises aside, preschool children are unreliable when it comes to the care of a pet. It would be easy, but probably inaccurate, to interpret this negligence as not caring. It is probably closer to the truth to say that children think of pets as belonging in the class of siblings. This puts the responsibility for their care clearly in the hands of the parents.

PLANTS

Although children as naturalists are especially interested in animals, they are also intrigued by things that grow, especially when they can be picked. Faria found a dandelion in the backyard and couldn't make up her mind whether or not to pick it.

Finally, she turned to her father, "Daddy, tell me, if I pick the flower off the plant is it still real?"

A preschool child's interest in flowers and plants goes beyond wanting to pick them. With an adult as a companion, preschool children often enjoy nature walks. They can look for moss growing on the shady side of rocks, clusters of tiny wild flowers, weeds with an interesting smell, or leaves that are turning colors. Children also enjoy a nature hunt where they gather up nuts and seed pods.

As children pursue their interest in plants and animals, the questions they ask can be difficult to answer. They expect that parents will know the name of every weed or wildflower. They want to know why cats eat birds, why kittens don't have daddies, and why dogs have to die before they're as old as mommy. Many of the questions that are described in the first section of this book are inspired by the young child's feeling of kinship with other living things.

COLLECTIONS

While preschool children love to play with plants and animals, they are equally fascinated with natural things that can be collected. Dennis loved to collect shells that he found near the beach. Rachel spent much of her time gathering acorns that fell in her yard.

Some children enjoy sorting out the items that they have collected. They may put leaves that look alike together, place the rocks with spots in one pile and the rocks without spots in another, or make a line of shells going from smallest to biggest. For most children, however, this sorting activity is short-lived. It is much more fun gathering shells, rocks, and leaves than sorting them into piles.

Peter and his father went for a walk to the creek. The walk took a very long time because Peter insisted on stopping every few seconds to pick up a stone or a pebble. As soon as they got home Peter took the stones out of his pocket. "Why don't we sort out the stones," his father suggested. "We could put all the white stones together and all the stones with lots of colors in a different pile." "Yeah, yeah, we'll sort our stones," Peter agreed.

Peter put all the stones on the kitchen table. "This is the Daddy stone," Peter explained, as he picked up one of the larger stones. He started talking to the stone. "You are the Daddy. Want to go see the creek? Hippety, hippety, here you go. Go fast, hippety hop. Find your boy. Here he is. Daddy, I want to go for a swim. OK, but watch out for the shark. Is that swim fun?"

Peter's father stopped trying to get his son to sort out the rocks. "Telling a story with the rocks," he told himself, "is a fine way of sorting stones." Peter's storytelling with the rocks is typical of many preschool children. For young children, the way to sort out rocks is to create a pretend story.

SUGGESTIONS FOR PARENTS

Although preschool children cannot be expected to take care of an animal or plant on a daily basis, they do love to participate in their care. Watering the plants, giving the dog a biscuit, or

sprinkling the fish food into the aquarium are usually prized activities. As long as we are careful not to scold a child for an occasional slipup, preschool children will continue to think of their chores with pets as both a responsibility and a privilege.

Children's fascination with animals and plants extends to the out-of-doors. Preschool children have a special sensitivity to natural beauty, especially on a small scale. They are intrigued with butterflies and bugs, lizards and snails, tiny flowers, rocks, acorns, and pine cones. Plan leisurely walks with your child so that you can share these miniature discoveries. Encourage your child to collect rocks and shells by providing nonbreakable containers in which to save these treasures.

As children pursue their scientific interests, parents will find that there are times when they are delighted with their children's curiosity and other times when they are upset by all the mess. The more exuberant a child becomes as he digs in the mud, chases after crawling things, and helps out in the kitchen, the more likely it is that parents will have to set limits. At the same time, parents need to think back to the questions that preschool children are asking about their world. As children actively observe, explore, and experiment with living and non-living things, they are finding out some of the answers in ways they can understand.

PLAY IDEAS

Most preschoolers enjoy seeing animals at a zoo. Before you arrange a trip to the zoo, read your child a book about zoo animals. Focus on five or six animals that you know you will find at the zoo. Visit the animals you have selected and take photos of them. As you go through your photo album with your child, talk about the special characteristics of the animals you visited. On the next trip to the zoo introduce your child to a few new animals. Make your zoo visit short and leisurely and your child will not be overwhelmed.

Give your child firsthand experience with growing things. Help him plant a seed and give it water and sunlight. Finger paint a pot for the plant, and let your child transplant it as soon as it begins to grow. Ask your child to give his plant a special name. Make lines on a craft stick using different colored markers. Place the craft stick in the pot with the plant to that your child can see how much the plant has grown.

Children are unlikely to be afraid of bugs unless they discover that their parents are afraid. Give your child an empty plastic bottle with holes in the lid. If she finds an ant or spider in the house, suggest that he let it crawl into the bottle. Talk about the bug. How many legs does it have? Does it have wings? What does it eat? Suggest to your child that she carry the insect outside so that it can play with its friends.

If you have a special tree in your yard, make a practice of going outside and visiting the tree at least once a week. Ask your child to talk about ways in which the tree is changing. Does it have buds or new leaves? Is fruit growing on the tree? What sort of noise does the tree make when the winds blows it? Do drops of water stay on the leaves after a rainstorm? Do the leaves change color in autumn? Do they fall off the tree? Give your child a turn to ask you questions about the ways the tree is changing. Put music on in the house and pretend with your child that he is a tree with branches that sway when the wind blows.

Help your child turn over a small rock. Is there moss on the rock? Are there bugs crawling underneath?

If you live near a farm that allows you to pick your own fruit, let your child help you pick or gather the fruits. When you get home, cut or peel the fruit, and discover with your child what the fruit looks like inside.

Take your child to the supermarket. See if she can help you find the different vegetables on your list.

Take a book about butterflies out of the library. Take your child to a butterfly farm and help him name some of the butterflies.

A visit to an aviary or an aquarium provides children with a special opportunity to enjoy watching living things. The more informed you are about the living things you visit, the more pleasure your child will get from each of your excursions.

Let your child take photos of flowers in your garden. When the photos are developed, go outside with your child and see if she can find the flowers that are in the photos.

Play twin hunt with your child. Put five or six items in a box: a leaf, a stone, an acorn, a piece of bark, a blade of grass, a twig. Go for a walk with your child. Can you find a "twin" for each item in the box?

After a rain or snow storm, see if you and your child can find paw prints. Talk about the prints. What kind of an animal made the prints? How big were the prints? In which direction was the animal going? Was he going straight or did he stop along the way?

Put some dirt in a flower pot. Let your child find "twigs" and plant them in a pot. Help him tear up some scraps of green paper. See if he would like to glue the "leaves" on the twigs.

Help your child gather icicles after a snow storm and put them in a paper cup. What happens to the icicles when she brings them into the house?

PLAYING SCHOOL

MARY HAD A LITTLE LAMB

Mary had a little lamb
Whose fleece was white as snow.
And everywhere that Mary went,
The lamb was sure to go.
It followed her to school one day
Which was against the rules.
It made the children laugh and play
To see a lamb at school.

On preschool orientation day, Miss Becky gave each child a paper Care Bear® with the child's name on it. "After today," Miss Becky explained, "you will come to school without your mommy. Put your Care Bear on the Bear Tree and Care Bear will watch out for you." When orientation was over, Luisa convinced her teacher to give her an extra Care Bear. With the help of the school secretary, she wrote her Nana's name on the Care Bear and stuck it under the tree in the classroom. On the way out she told her mother, "Nana is coming to school with me. I put her name under the tree." At three years old, Luisa, like other preschool children, ascribed a certain magic power to numbers and letters. A Care Bear with Nana's name would bring Nana to school and keep both of them safe.

"Playing School" includes three chapters: "Word Play," "Learning to Read," and "Playing With Numbers." In "Word Play," we describe children's fascination in reading letters and writing words. In "Learning to Read," we talk about how children listen to stories, pretend to read, and learn to read for real. In "Playing With Numbers," we look at children's fascination with counting, and their emerging ability to put objects in a sequence or arrange objects in sets. The suggestions for parents at the end of each chapter describe ways of supporting children's growing interest in readiness skills without taking away their spirit of adventure.

CHAPTER 10

Word Play

~~~~~~

ELETELEPHONY

Once there was an elephant
Who tried to use the telephant—
No! No! I mean an elephone
Who tried to use the telephone.
(Dear me! I am not certain quite
That even now I've got it right.)
Howe'er it was, he got his trunk
Entangled in the telephunk.
The more he tried to get it free
The louder buzzed the telephee.
(I fear I'd better drop the song
Of elephop and telephong!)

—Laura E. Richards

Caroline, at three years old, was a regular fan of "Sesame Street." She loved watching the letters of the alphabet pop onto the screen and could name almost every one. Two years later, when Caroline entered kindergarten, she was reading books. Caroline's parents were convinced that her precocious reading could be attributed to "Sesame Street."

Caroline's achievement, however, is not typical of most children. Children who learn to name letters at an early age will not necessarily read early. Some children do make steady progress—from naming letters to sounding out words to read-

~~~

ing books—but for most children this progression is neither quick nor steady. Fortunately, with few exceptions, children who have good language skills and who enjoy having books read to them become good readers in elementary school. On the other hand, children who are drilled in reading before they show a spontaneous interest may develop negative feelings about the skill. It is much more productive to teach preschool children how to enjoy books than to teach them how to read.

In this chapter, we look at ways in which children in the preschool years lay the groundwork for reading and writing. The first section focuses on children's ability to sound out and recognize words. In the second section, we examine their ability to interpret messages. In the third section, we talk about writing skills. We look at how children use their interest in written messages as a bridge to learning to read. The final section of the chapter is devoted to computer programs that expose children to reading in ways that are fun and open-ended.

RECOGNIZING LETTERS AND WORDS

As the sky-writing plane passed overhead, three-year-old Brenda stared in amazement. The words "VISIT CLAM BAKERS" were stretched across the horizon. "Mommy, Mommy, look, my B is up there!"

The sequence in which children learn words is fairly predictable. Generally, the first word they recognize is their own name and they feel quite possessive about all of its letters. Next, they are likely to turn their interest to logos. Parents have reported that their two- and three-year-olds can recognize the names of fast-food restaurants or the labels on cereal boxes. Although children may focus on shape and color rather than the sequence of letters to identify a logo, this spontaneous sign reading is impressive.

Parents who believe in formal reading instruction for preschoolers may introduce flash cards as a way of building sight vocabulary. Occasionally a child will really enjoy these flash cards and master an impressive stack of words. More often, children learn a word one day and forget it completely the next. Learning to attach the right words to a stack of cardboard cards doesn't have the same appeal as identifying a McDonald's restaurant or finding the box of cereal o's on the pantry shelf.

While some parents use a flash-card approach to teach early word reading, other parents focus on teaching alphabet skills. They may begin by teaching their child to name and identify the letters of the alphabet, or they may try to teach phonics skills by concentrating on the sounds that letters make. For example, Brenan and his mother like to play rhyming games. "I'm swinging in the leaves!" Brenan called one day as he swung on a rope and landed in a leaf pile. His mother countered, "I'm singing in the leaves, and bringing in the leaves."

"I'm flinging in the leaves," added Brenan, as he playfully flung some at his mother. The game continued with jumping, bumping, thumping; dancing, prancing; skipping, dipping, dripping, tipping; and throwing and blowing.

Whichever route a parent takes, there are complications. Letters make different sounds in different words, and upper-case letters look different from lower-case letters. Hal had learned to identify the letters in his name in upper case. When his aunt wrote his name in lower-case letters, Hal came running to his mother. "Do you know what Aunt Caroline did? She took the foot off my L!"

Even if a child is successful in learning the different sounds and shapes of all the letters, there is a long road ahead before they learn to read words. The first challenge to master is

sound blending or stringing the sounds together. A child may sound out "CAT" (C-A-T) without a flaw and still not know that the word he is sounding out is cat. Gretchen painstakingly sounded out the letters in "animal." When her mother asked her what word she was reading, Gretchen was quite put out. "I already read the word," Gretchen insisted. "A-N-I-M-A-L." A second problem that children face is the irregularity of the English language. The more common a word is, the less likely it is to follow phonetic rules. Think about the words in this sentence: "Two girls were in the house." How many of the words in this sentence are phonetic?

Despite the many difficulties involved with phonics, some preschool children become adept at identifying the words that they sound out. Although parents are justifiably pleased when their children make this kind of breakthrough, word identification cannot be equated with reading.

INTERPRETING MESSAGES

Katie learned that a row of words could carry an important message. Her mother took advantage of this interest and wrote Katie notes on the napkin in her lunch box that the teacher would help her read. After lunch one day her teacher insisted that all the children throw away their napkins. "No, I can't," Katie insisted. "My mommy wrote me a letter." For Katie these notes from her mother were more than a reading activity. They were a way to stay connected when her mother was not there.

There is a watershed separation between reading words and reading messages. In order to understand a written message, children must recognize how the words they read are related to each other. Even children with good phonic skills may be unable to read a complete sentence. The small words like "the" and "are" that connect the nouns and the verbs are likely to be irregular. When children try to sound them out, they lose the sense of the sentence.

Children who have learned to read by a "sight-say" method may also have difficulty with function words but for a different reason. Four-year-old Meling, who had trouble remembering the flash card with the word "the," sheds some light on the problem. "Mommy," she asked one day, "what does a 'the' look like?"

Although many preschoolers don't learn to read despite their parents best efforts, some preschoolers learn to read with ease. These early readers have certain characteristics in common. They enjoy listening to stories and are good conversationalists. They have parents who enjoy reading and who provide them with a selection of attractive books. The parents are available to answer questions, but do not drill or quiz their child. In other words, parents of children who are early readers have

created a climate that encourages their child to read for enjoyment.

Recognizing that reading is an advanced skill, parents often ask whether they should search for or avoid a preschool that teaches reading. The important distinction is not whether a preschool teaches reading, but how. Schools that emphasize rote learning are likely to be less interesting for children. Schools that provide many opportunities for children to look at books, hear stories, play with plastic letters, incorporate "reading" and "writing" into pretend play, use wall charts and signs, and see their own words in print are likely to be both more fun and more successful.

WRITING LETTERS AND WORDS

While some children are more interested than others in learning the names of letters, almost every child is fascinated by writing. In the beginning, writing is a kind of pretending. Children make some squiggles on a piece of paper and ask their

parent to read what they have written. Although children know that their squiggles are not real writing, it doesn't detract from the fun of these conversational games.

Children who begin with squiggles very often go on to forming real letters. Naturally, the first letters that they form are the letters in their own name, and the first word they write is their name. Their interest in reading and writing tends to follow the same sequence: from letters to words to messages. However, children are usually interested in writing messages before they have mastered reading books.

Children who want to write messages pursue this interest in different ways. Some think up messages and ask their parents to write them out. Others laboriously write out a message by asking their parents to dictate to them one letter at a time. Once they have written out a message, they read it out loud.

USING A COMPUTER TO READ AND WRITE

Writing letters, for a preschooler, is a tedious task and they quite naturally look for shortcuts. An obvious shortcut is to begin with ready-made letters. Brenan liked to arrange plastic letters on the refrigerator door. By paying attention to the commercials on television, he discovered that letters put in order make a word. One morning, after watching a commercial, he lined up the letters J-E-L-L-O. "I did it," he announced proudly, "I wrote Jell-O. "

Brenan loved to write words by arranging plastic letters on the refrigerator. As his writing vocabulary increased, however, he always ran out of just the letter he needed. When he wrote "daddy" on the refrigerator, he didn't have a "d" left for "dog." Fortunately he discovered the computer. The computer had an

infinite number of letters that never looked upside down and always stayed on the line. "I wrote a letter," Brenan boasted to his Dad. "It says ball, baby, boat, and Brenan, and I didn't even run out of Bs."

Sarah Rose, at three, loved to fill the computer screen with random letters. She was especially thrilled when she learned how to print out her "letter," which she gleefully "read" to anyone who would listen. Educators recognize this pretend writing and reading as an important step toward real or conventional reading and writing. Arran, at four, loved to write names. His mother would set the font size at 24 points and push the "caps lock" button. Then, with prompting, Arran would carefully write the names of all the people in his family. He soon learned how to spell and write the names himself. Chen's favorite activity was making birthday cards. With the help of his mother he learned how to use Print Shop® and insisted on making a card for everyone in his family.

Children who like having their favorite stories read to them are often especially attracted to computer "storybooks." At two and a half, Jordan learned how to activate his Dr. Seuss ABC Book program and move from page to page. Jordan especially liked the fact that the "puter" was never too tired or to busy to read the book with him six times in a row.

For older preschool children, interactive "storybooks" can provide enjoyable support for learning to read. Most interactive storybook programs encourage children to interact with the story on several levels: they can hear the narrative, make characters talk, explore details in the pictures, activate animations that enhance the story, and even retell the story in their own way. There is a lot to talk about with a parent or friend, especially when there are supplementary activities with choices to make. For example, after hearing and playing out "The Princess and the Pea," Arran chose an activity in which he dressed the prince and princess for their wedding. He then added a unique ending to the tale: "So they put on their hats and their mittens and went outside to throw snowballs."

Interactive storybooks can also direct children's attention to text. Many highlight words as they are read, or enable children to click on words to activate animations. Others encourage children to predict the text by hiding the words until the text button is clicked. Pierre, who was learning to read in kindergarten, proudly told us what was happening on each page of his new interactive storybook. He would then play the text for us, showing us the words that the computer was reading. When the words didn't quite match his prediction, he would point out the discrepancy.

Writing your own words is one of the most effective ways to learn to read. Research shows that children who work out the phonetic system themselves by struggling to represent the sounds they hear become better readers than those who learn only by recognizing words. Computers can be very helpful in this process. Children tend to write more on computers than by hand because they like the way their writing looks. Many children's word processors and book-making programs contain helpful starters, such as small rebus pictures that can be "stamped" into a line of text and switched back and forth between picture and word. Text-to-speech features allow children to hear what they have written, even when they use idiosyncratic spelling. It's fun to hear the robot voice reading back the words, and many children improve their spelling with this feedback.

Caroline's transition to reading was unusually rapid, but the process she went through was typical of many children. For months, Caroline had been making "books" by folding paper and putting a drawing and some letters on each "page." Her letter combinations had been getting closer and closer to real words, but she couldn't yet read unfamiliar material or write recognizable words without being told how to spell them. Her older brothers had dominated the computer. Caroline's aunt, uncle, and older cousins came for Christmas, bringing a book-making program with rebus pictures and text-to-speech. For the entire weekend, Caroline monopolized both the computer and the visitors. With both assistance and a captive audience, she wrote and played back countless stories about a girl named Caroline and the things she liked to do. By the end of the week-end, Caroline was reading!

SUGGESTIONS FOR PARENTS

From a very early age, children love to have people read to them. In some families, the practice of reading a bedtime story continues through the preschool years. In other families, the practice peters out as parents get busy with younger siblings or children become independent about bedtime. Although parents may not want to read to their preschool children at a set time, reading to children on a daily basis is a good practice.

While we do not recommend flash cards and commercial reading-readiness workbooks, there are many prereading games that parents and children can enjoy. Some of these games help children tune into the sound system of language. Other games capitalize on their interest in writing.

Games with Sounds

Learning to recognize rhyming words sensitizes children to differences in vowel sounds. More importantly, most children have fun with rhyming words. In addition to reading poems and rhyming books, parents and children can invent their own rhyming games.

As your child gets dressed in the morning or puts away his or her toys, invent a silly poem and let her put in the rhyming word:

> *I wonder what you're going to do.*
> *I think you will put on your* _____ .
> *I see something over there.*
> *I think it is your teddy* _____ .

A second way to tune children into letter sounds is to play games with first-letter sounds. The preschool practice of having a letter of the week can be carried out at home. On B day, for instance, you might want to find a picture of a butterfly, let bear and Big Bird join you for breakfast, and serve beans and bacon for dinner. A less elaborate game involves making up alliteration sentences: "Susie saw a silly salamander sitting in the sun."

Games with Letters

Children are intrigued by letters and enjoy incorporating them into their games. If you have a set of alphabet blocks or magnetic letters, try writing out your child's name, leaving a space for a missing letter. Your child will enjoy the challenge of finding the missing letter and putting it in place. For the child who is interested in spelling out simple words, play beginner's Draw-a-Man. Like regular Hangman, the goal of the game is to guess the letters of the word before a stick figure of a man is completed. (Every time the player guesses a letter that is not in the word, one body part is added to the stick figure.) For beginner's Draw-a-Man, tell your child the word before the game begins. Then, when she guesses a letter that is in the word, place the letter in the correct spot on the word line.

Roll out sheets of modeling clay and let your child stamp

letters, words, or messages with plastic letters. These clay letters can be decorated with buttons, beads, raisins, or other small objects.

Play alphabet hunt games when you go on outings. You can look for lots of examples of a particular letter, find all the letters in your child's name, or find the letters of the alphabet in order. (Played cooperatively, this is a great way to keep children busy on long car trips.)

Point out letter formations, words, or letter combinations that you think might intrigue your child. For example, show her how your name looks in the fancy writing on a wedding invitation and the plain print on a bill. If your child is beginning to recognize and sound out words, you might point out the "tree" in "street," the "rip" in "trip," or the "jam" in "pajamas." Find letters and words on license plates, or collect examples of words like "spaghetti," "encyclopedia," and "supercalifragilisticexpealidocious" that are hard (but fun) to say.

Choose books that emphasize word play, such as *There's a Wocket in My Pocket* by Dr. Seuss. Encourage your child to read portions aloud with you. After you've finished the book, talk together about the words and phrases you liked. Can your child think up some similar ones of her own?

Encourage your child to make "books" or scrapbooks by providing folded paper or using a book-making computer program. Children can put a picture and some letters or words on each "page."

Read your child's favorite books together. Track the words with your fingers as you read. Point out one or two interesting words, such as the name of the main character or a word your child likes to repeat. Give your child a turn to "read" a page he has memorized. Can he point to words as he reads? Can he find a favorite word?

Interpreting and Sending Messages

Look for picture books that tell a story without words. Encourage your child to tell a story to go with the pictures.

Work with your child on a photo album about herself or about a special event. Have your child dictate a caption for each picture.

Keep paper and pencil in play areas, to encourage spontaneous "writing."

Once your child is familiar with the way letters look and sound, he or she is likely to become interested in reading and writing messages. Children who like to write enjoy sending out short letters and party invitation, exchanging notes with a parent, or making up shopping lists. (Don't correct their spelling! It takes the fun out of writing.) For children who are more interested in reading messages, ask them to describe their drawings and write out the description, tack messages on the refrigerator, put short notes in their lunch box, or play a treasure-hunt game using word clues.

Write a letter or postcard to your child and mail it. Your child will love getting mail! She may even want to send some herself.

Make a family message center, where you can leave notes for each other and keep track of important appointments, phone numbers, and other messages. Encourage your preschooler to contribute drawings and messages.

Help your child make "important" signs, such as "SAVE" (to put on block structures), a name tag for a pet's cage or bowl, a welcome sign or "This is_____'s house" sign to put on the front door when a new friend comes over, a "happy birthday" banner, or a label for a special keepsake box or secret hideout.

Make a short list of your child's favorite relatives' and friends' names and phone numbers and post it near the phone.

Encourage your child to help you find the right number when it is time to call, or even to call the number himself.

Make books of your child's favorite bedtime stories. Write a few sentences on each page, and have your child illustrate them. Can she put the pages in order? Can she tell you what is happening on each one?

Using Computers

There are a number of ways to use computers to build on children's fascination with letters and words. Perhaps the simplest is to enlarge the type on a standard word processing program. At first, your child may enjoy filling the page with random letters, printing out his "note," and "reading" you what it says. As he learns how letters combine to form words, he may enjoy working with you to type lists of family names or favorite words, or to type out simple messages.

Some children enjoy writing in color. This can be done with many adult and children's word processors, and also with painting programs that have a text feature.

Help your child to use the computer to make signs, labels, cards, and posters to organize her things, adorn her block structures, or enhance her pretend play. Many children especially enjoy using programs that enable them to make banners, award certificates, greeting cards, or gifts.

Get computer versions of your child's favorite storybooks, or storybook versions of computer books that he likes. What differences does your child notice between the two versions? Does he have a preference for one style of reading the text? After playing the computer version, can he "read" some of the text pages himself? Can he point out any of the words?

Many children get a special thrill from seeing their words in print. Type up your child's questions, spontaneous poems, and descriptions of her drawings, or have her dictate "stories" to you.

Choose computer programs that encourage your child to make up stories of his own, or to tell familiar stories in his own way. Encourage your child to use these with a friend, sibling, or you. You can collaborate on each page, or take turns. Print out some of the stories, and encourage your child to make a cover page. Keep these published books in a special place. Find time to read them to your child, and to let him "read" them to others in the family.

Encourage your child to make captioned pictures, cards, and storybooks to give as gifts to friends and relatives.

Introduce your child to e-mail. Send and receive messages together. To send e-mail to your child, write "for (your child's name)" as the "subject" and send the mail to your family address.

CHAPTER 11

Story Telling

~~~~~~~~~~~~~~~~~~~~~~~~~~~~~~~~~~~

PICTURE BOOKS IN WINTER

Summer fading, winter comes,
Frosty mornings, tingling thumbs.
Window robins, winter rooks,
and the picture story books.

—Robert Louis Stevenson

Because the role of storyteller is a difficult one, it is natural for young children to concentrate initially on the role of listener. Learning to appreciate a story, in fact, is a considerable challenge for preschool children. For some preschool children, the challenge lies in making connections between the spoken words and the illustrations. Preschool children who recognize the connection between the illustrations and the spoken words may still have difficulty following the story line. "Daddy," Mason insisted, "Don't read that page. It doesn't have a picture."

LISTENING TO STORIES

Whatever its complexity, the attraction of a story is its power to arouse emotions. The stories that appeal most to children are built on themes that are exciting, scary, or adventurous. Fairy tales and folk tales are traditional favorites. The plots of these

~~~

stories are likely to be scary, but inevitably the ending is happy and a child turns into the hero.

Stories with monsters, scary giants, dangerous animals, or evil parents have a strong appeal. In *Jack in the Beanstalk*, Jack climbs up a beanstalk and unexpectedly encounters an evil giant. In *Little Red Riding Hood*, the sick grandmother turns out to be a deceptive and hungry wolf. In *Hansel and Gretel*, the children are confronted by an evil witch who tries to cook them in an oven.

Less scary and traditional stories appeal to children's senses of humor and help them feel superior. Children love the Winnie the Pooh stories, where the hero is a lovable bear of very little brain and a very big heart. They love many of the nursery rhymes that are silly or absurd.

The emotional appeal of these fairy tales for preschool children is that they speak to real fears. The children are concerned about being attacked by animals with sharp teeth or being threatened by angry and malevolent parents. Feeling strong enough to protect yourself, through the vicarious experience of a story, is reassuring.

In recent years, a third theme has become more noticeable. Many stories are focusing on feelings that are part of intimate relationships. There are stories about making and losing friends, about feeling sad when someone dies, about feeling jealous of a new baby. Preschool children are interested in exploring these feelings by listening to stories. Their desire to empathize with others and to be caring is stimulated.

Good stories tend to produce a variety of feelings in both adults and children. Such stories, like people, are emotionally complex. Parents and children can explore their feelings of accomplishment, amusement, and empathy when they share these stories.

Kenneth was spending the night with his grandmother. After reading three storybooks that Kenneth had selected, she decided to put out the light. "But, Nana," Kenneth pleaded, "you promised to tell me a story."

Although reading a book to a child takes less effort than telling a story, it is never quite the same. Stories invented for your child and told in your own words create feelings of closeness and intimacy that a storybook reading can't match. Parents who spend the extra moments to tell their child a bedtime story are well rewarded. As they share fantasies and wishes with their children, they strengthen the parent-child bond and store up special memories that they will always treasure.

STORIES THAT CHILDREN TELL

When preschool children begin to recite a favorite story word for word, turning the pages at just the right moment, they are indicating that they want to assume the role of storyteller. Although their performance is not true storytelling, it does help them become aware of how stories are structured. Stories have their own logic in which the characters are developed, the central problem is resolved, and a final theme emerges. There are many variations, of course, on this basic story structure, but until children have internalized these elements they cannot tell coherent stories.

When children go beyond memorization and describe what they see happening in the pictures of a book, they are coming closer to storytelling. Typically, however, these descriptions do not add up to a unified story line. Children may begin with comments that connect the first few pictures, but then they suddenly switch focus and pick up another idea. Similarly, preschool children make up charming songs and monologues that include connected images but not a coherent story line. Amelia, sitting inside the sandbox, made up a story as she wiggled her toes in the sand.

When I take off my shoes,
I wiggle them like a worm.
My toes are saying gobble, gobble.
They are a turkey, like a bunny—
See those two little ears.
This is Mickey Mouse
And he wiggles like a worm.
Mickey Mouse, with his big fat ears,
And his face is round.
And he wiggles like a worm.

The most polished stories are told by children as they pretend with small-scale toys. We call this kind of storytelling "producer-director" play. Like the producer-director of a film or drama, the child tells the story by controlling the actions of a cast of characters. The cast may be dolls, robots, toy animals, or even miniature cars. Assuming the detached perspective of the producer-director, the child animates the characters by speaking for them in a high squeaky voice, as he makes the character who is doing the talking jump up and down.

Allison is playing with her miniature characters. She picks up a monster and makes him pop up and down. "Me wants a cookie—me hungry—me going to find a cookie." Next, Allison

picks up a hippopotamus. "Grr, grr, grunt—go away. You can't
have any cookies. They're my cookies." Allison picks up the
monster again. "I'm hungry. Me gets all the cookies. Mmm,
this cookie tastes good. Me wants more cookies."

In producer-director play, theatrical devices help children
tell the story. It is not necessary to describe the story's setting,
for it is apparent from the arrangement of toys. As the characters speak, the producer/director moves them up and down,
thereby eliminating the need for phrases like "she said" or "he
asked." Likewise, transitions between events can be demonstrated by manipulating the toys rather than through narration.
The children are free to concentrate on the dialogue, and when
two children work together, each one taking a different role, the
dialogue can carry a recognizable story line:

Veronica (holding a Mickey Mouse character): Hello, Donald. Ready for the Mickey Mouse Revue?
Davita (holding Donald Duck): No, I can't come, I lost my drumstick.
Veronica: Well, you better find it. The parade has got to get started.
Davita: The dragon eated it up.
Veronica: You got bad trouble!

Preschool children who have a special gift for storytelling may progress to the point of producing original stories without props. Even then, however, their stories are more like a series of snapshots than a continuous flow of events. Nicholas, after a hurricane warning, told the following original story:

"There was a hurricane over the house. A hand came down and picked Nicholas up by the hair. He cut the hand off, and it fell to the ground. He took the hand to jail."

More commonly, preschool children show they are on their way to original storytelling by adding a new bit to a familiar story. Celia created an original version of *Goldilocks and the Three Bears:*

"Then Goldilocks took a bite of Momma Bear's porridge. She said, 'This is too yucky!' and she ran out of the bear's house and her mommy took her to McDonald's and all the bears went home, and Momma Bear said 'Who ate my porridge?' The end."

Like other kinds of imaginative play, the stories a child tells, whatever the form, reveal that child's feelings. By watching and listening we can glimpse their wishes, fears, and joys. Brenan, at five years old, is celebrating a sunny day:

It's not the leaves.
It's not the rakes.
It's the sun of the morn.
Just don't put on your sunglasses
Just go out into the sun of the morn.

Just play in the leaves
Your father raked for you.
It's fun in the sun of the morn.

THE EXTRA STORYTELLER

Television is the extra storyteller in every family, and its versatility is growing with the appearance of new cable channels and video cassettes. Children are exposed to an overwhelming number of stories through television. This form of storytelling has the disadvantage of being less controlled by the children. They cannot stop and talk about part of a story nor skip a scary event. Once they have been scared by a television show, they may refuse to watch it again. On the other hand, television storytelling can be exceptionally powerful as far as arousing emotion. Because it is a visual medium in which close-ups of the human face appear constantly, the viewer's attention is directed toward body language and facial expressions.

Clearly, television viewing influences the attitudes of young children. Watching violent programming, even cartoons, results in more aggressive play and, perhaps, a more accepting attitude toward violence. By contrast, watching programs about minority children or about foreign countries results in a more accepting attitude toward differences in people.

While some children's shows are fine for children to watch, an overdose of even good television can have negative effects. Some children get so glued to the television set they have little time for interactive play. It is clearly better for children to listen to a story told or read by a parent than to spend their valuable time watching a television show.

SUGGESTIONS FOR PARENTS

Since storytelling begins with listening, parents can help their children get started by reading them interesting books. Most public libraries have large collections of picture books with suitable stories for preschoolers. If possible, it is a good idea to plan on at least half an hour of browsing in order to select the ones you really like. Preschool children usually grab the first books they see, which can result in dull or inappropriate stories. Let your child pick a few books and then look at them in the library while you select additional books more carefully. A children's librarian can be very helpful in suggesting particular authors and illustrators which your child might enjoy.

In choosing books for your child, think about the following qualities:

- How well is the book illustrated? Children enjoy looking at pictures as much as listening to words. They enjoy beauty, humor, and fantasy. Avoid books where the illustrations are too busy or over-stylized.
- Does the book match your child's listening skills? Do not go by age. Choose a story that is complex enough to capture your child's interest but easy enough to follow.
- Is this a book that your child will enjoy? Don't be over-concerned with educational value. Any story that your child enjoys is educationally valid.
- Does the story have emotional appeal? Although children enjoy informational books, stories that qualify as longtime favorites appeal to a child's emotions.
- Is the book well written? Children tune into the sound of language as well as its meaning. Be especially wary of books that are marked "easy reading." They may be easy to read, but very dull to listen to.
- Does the book appeal to you? When you read a book to your

child that you really like, the chances are very good that your child will like it too.

What if your child isn't interested in books and won't sit still to listen to a story? Here are four ways to approach the problem:

- Stimulate the child's interest in pictures. Most books for young children have many pictures, and if your child becomes sufficiently interested in the pictures, listening to the stories will follow naturally. Find out which pictures attract your child and talk about them. Pictures are everywhere: in books, painting, posters, billboards, signs, photographs. Perhaps your child would like more activity—cut and paste pictures from magazines.
- Tantalize your child with reading. Choose a book you think will interest your child, sit down alone, and read the book loudly to yourself. Be sure to sit in a spot that is convenient for the child to join you.
- Show your own enjoyment of reading by spending time each day with your own books or magazines. Children who see their parents read are likely to want to do the same.
- Try the appeal of high-tech reading. Buy a book with an accompanying cassette tape and show your child how to operate the tape recorder. If your child prefers listening to stories on the tape recorder, you can easily record other picture books. Your child may also enjoy computer story-books. Once he learns how to "turn the pages" on the computer, he will "read" his favorite stories over and over again.

Look for computer storybooks that encourage children to interact with the story by making characters talk and act out their parts, activating animations that enhance the story, choosing what happens next, helping characters accomplish their goals, or retelling the story in their own way. To stimulate conversation about the story and the choices the computer offers, work with your child at the computer or encourage him to play with a sibling or friend.

Reading storybooks provides many opportunities to encourage your child to become an active participant, to join in the storytelling. Naturally, it is fun to pause and talk about the pictures. Look for surprises or incongruities in the pictures. Illustrators seem to enjoy adding private jokes to their pictures. Perhaps a detail you find will suggest a new twist to the plot, such as a mouse who looks sad when everyone else in the picture is happy. Try going beyond the information in the picture: "I wonder who lives in this tree? Where do you think that car is going in such a hurry?"

When reading a story for the first time, you and your child can sometimes guess what's going to come next before you turn the page. If your child likes to make guesses, stop midway through the story and try to predict how it will end. This technique, which also can be used with television programs, is an excellent way to help your child become more aware of story structure.

Because you can read the book and your child cannot, conversations about a story can sometimes seem like quizzes to the child. One way to soften your authoritative position is to use a puppet. As you read the story, the puppet breaks in with comments and questions. Conversely, your child can hold the puppet. Then your comments will be directed to a puppet who may be more willing to respond.

In your conversations about a story, remember the potential of stories is to highlight human motivation. You can question a character's emotional state: "I guess she's getting madder and madder." You can compare yourself to a character: "I wouldn't do that because it's too dangerous," or invite your child to make such a comparison. You can place yourself and your child directly in the story: "I'm not scared of that tiger;

I'm going to stand on this rock. Where are you going to stand?"

The purpose of all these techniques is to make story reading like storytelling. The activity becomes more fun for both you and your child as the two of you add your imaginative power to that of the author. Soon you will gain confidence in your ability to tell stories and may not need the book at all. If you still feel a bit unsure about your own storytelling, try one of the play ideas below.

PLAY IDEAS

Tell a "story" that recaps an experience from the past. You can recount what you or your child did yesterday or retell a special event from the recent past. Change some of the details or provide a surprise ending.

Build a story from a book that you and your child have enjoyed. Describe the further adventures of the main characters. Perhaps you can imagine them visiting your family.

Tell a story that is based on one of your child's drawings. Think about the objects your child likes to draw and weave them into a story.

As you experiment with storytelling, involve your child in the process. Preschool children enjoy defining the characters: thinking up names for them, deciding whether they live in a big house or a little house, and so on. At the end, they like to choose a happy ending or a sad ending.

You can also help your child tell a story through producer-director play. You can encourage the play to start by asking your child to tell you the names of the characters (whether they are miniature dolls, toy robots, or some other kind of toy). You can ask what the characters are going to do or suggest that one of the characters wants to do a particular thing. You can even assume a role and help create the dialogue.

CHAPTER 12

Numbers

I counted all my cookies.
I counted up to 10.
But if I take another one,
I'll have to count again!

—M. Segal

Yoko: One, two, three, five, seven: Here I come, ready or not—
Cheng: No, Yoko, count one, two, three, four, five. Then you say, "Here I come, ready or not."
Yoko (imitating her brother's intonation): One, two, three, five, seven: Here I come, ready or not.

Yoko was attracted to the idea of counting, but despite her brother's careful tutoring, she couldn't reproduce the correct sequence. Like Yoko, most three-year-olds recite numbers in some sort of order, but they tend to skip over a number or two or say some numbers out of order. Counting by rote, which is emphasized by parents and preschool teachers alike, is only one part of the quantitative understanding that children acquire during the preschool period. During these years, children also learn to recognize sets and count rationally. They learn the meaning of comparative terms: more, same, less, bigger, stronger, and faster. Some preschool children with a fascination for numbers learn to add and subtract as well.

COUNTING

Jennifer, at two years old, liked to create a Disneyworld parade with her blocks and toy zoo animals. She would make a row of blocks and line up three animals on each block. Like Jennifer, many young children show an awareness of sets before they begin to count systematically. Gradually, small sets are associ-

ated with numbers. The children learn that they have two eyes, two hands, and two feet. Perhaps they learn that there are five fingers on each hand and five toes on each foot or that a dog has four feet and a car has four wheels. The ability to associate numbers with sets is often reflected in children's early drawings. Katie drew a picture of herself with a line of mammoth fingers emanating from stick-style arms.

At the same time, very young children start paying attention to the number sequence. Mark's favorite way of being carried to bed was on his father's shoulders. Every night, his father recited the same rhyme:

> *One, two, three, four.*
> *Here we are at Markie's door.*
> *Five, six, seven, eight.*
> *Go to sleep. It's getting late.*

Before long, Mark was counting for his teddy bear as he carried him on his shoulders to bed.

By the beginning of the preschool period, these two early accomplishments, set recognition and rote counting, start to come together. Most three-year-olds realize that the number sequence is used to count the quantity in a set. Counting accurately is a different matter. A child who counts only to five cannot accurately count ten objects. Accuracy is further diminished when numbers are skipped or out of order. Most fundamentally, counting cannot be accurate until a child assigns one and only one number to each object in a set.

The principle of one-to-one correspondence is the basis for rational counting. In trying to count

KATIE MASI

a set of objects, young preschoolers usually show a general appreciation of one-to-one correspondence but not a precise understanding. Children move their fingers from one object to another and recite the number sequence; in general they recite one number for each object. But from time to time, they will assign two numbers to a single object or pass over an object altogether. They either don't notice this lack of consistency or consider it to be of little consequence. The bottom line is that the children's final answers are often about right rather than exactly right.

By the end of the preschool period, most children understand one-to-one correspondence precisely enough to count small sets of objects accurately. They also can make two sets equal. "You have three cookies," Marcus's mother told him. "Your sister only has two. How many more cookies does she need so both of you will have the same?" Although this kind of question requires nothing more than counting, it assumes the form of an addition problem. Without being aware of it, Marcus is exploring the fact that $2 + 1 = 3$. Preschool children who can count accurately are ready for other counting activities that involve addition and subtraction. "Four people will be eating dinner. I put one fork on the table already. How many more should I get?"

Despite preschool children's increased skills, counting generally remains a rigid routine rather than a logical system they can decipher. Katerina, a five-year-old who loved to count, tried one day to count the number of stairs to her bedroom. Interrupted when she was nearly at the top, she came back down the stairs and started with "one." At first her parents interpreted this behavior as a clever stalling tactic, but later they noticed the same thing happening in other situations. Even if they tried to help by reminding her where she left off, Katerina could not pick up a counting sequence in the middle. Numbers were not yet a logical system that could be accessed at various points.

Even when five-year-olds become adept at counting, they can make mistakes that are surprising to adults. Having agreed that two rows have ten pennies each, and therefore the same amount, a child may change his or her answer when one row is spread out or bunched together. The two rows of pennies no longer look alike, and the child jumps to the conclusion that they no longer have the same number of pennies. If the problem is simplified by using one set of objects, similar results are likely. First, the child counts the line of pennies and gives the correct answer, "Ten." Then the pennies are placed in a stack, which looks quite different from the line, and the child is asked how many pennies there are now. Instead of answering immediately (no pennies have been added or removed), the child counts the stack of pennies all over again.

The realization that quantity is independent of appearance is called number conservation. Most preschoolers, even those who are good counters, have difficulty with number conservation.

Mason arranged his toy cars in a row and counted them one by one. "I have ten cars," he announced proudly. His father, who was curious about his son's knowledge of numbers, pushed the cars together and challenged his son to recount. Mason scowled at his father. "Why did you do that? Now I don't got ten anymore."

MEASUREMENT

Although preschool children have a marvelous time going around the house with a yardstick pretending to measure everything, they are unlikely to grasp the concept of measurement. Measurement is a complex form of counting in which continuous units, rather than objects, are counted. Moreover,

the units are, to all appearances, arbitrary. There is no discernable reason why length is measured in inches or weight in pounds.

Whatever the given unit, the secret to accurate measurement is keeping that unit consistent. It is this principle that is beyond the understanding of preschool children. Given a handful of cardboard footprints, they will be happy to measure how many "feet" it is from the kitchen to the bathroom. Of course, they will be unconcerned about carefully lining up the footprints so that each measured unit is equal. In effect, the children will treat the activity as one in which a series of footprints are counted. This is the kind of counting they understand.

Despite their inability to measure accurately, preschool children are learning three basic ideas about measurement. First, they are learning comparative terms that are used to measure things in a perceptual, nonquantitative manner. Many preschool children develop a rich vocabulary of these terms: bigger/ smaller, longer/ shorter, faster/slower, older/younger, heavier/lighter.

Second, the children are learning to associate the names of certain units with the attributes that they measure. The children become aware that pounds refer to weight, inches to length, and miles per hour to speed. This process of association is not without its comic side:

Carina (as cashier):You gotta put your stuff up here so I can ring it up. This is going to cost you lots of money.
Mother (as customer): Don't forget to weigh the apples.
Carina: I did. They weigh fifteen cents.

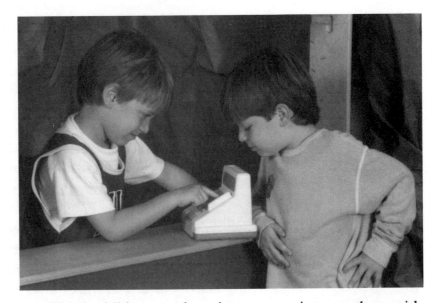

Third, children are learning to associate numbers with units of measurement. Michael's understanding of weight was superficial, but he knew that he weighed fifty-two pounds. In the same way, Rosita knew her mom was thirty-four years old even though the duration of a year was obscure. Davita found out that the speed limit in town was thirty miles per hour, and that her parents drove sixty miles per hour on the freeway. These bits of information are important, for they help children eventually integrate their knowledge of numbers into a measurement system.

USING COMPUTERS TO TEACH MATH

As with letter recognition and reading programs, early math programs come in several varieties. Some are quiz programs that reward correct answers, some are open-ended environments in which children can make their own counting books and other math stories, and the best combine a creative exploratory approach with features that help children learn spatial and mathematical concepts. For example, the child might make silly creatures by adding eyes, noses, mouths, antennae, etc. The child can ask for a specific number of parts, or place parts one at a time. As each part is added, an appealing robot voice states how many of that part there are. Other programs capitalize on children's interest in money, and help them count out coins and make change. Many provide interesting logical problems, shape puzzles, or experiences with one-to-one correspondence such as giving every bunny a carrot. The programs are designed to help the child succeed at the task; many also allow for open-ended play.

SUGGESTIONS FOR PARENTS

On "Sesame Street," Count Von Count loves numbers. Preschool children share the Count's love of numbers when counting is made a part of everyday experiences. Perhaps the most common example is counting food.

Children enjoy counting out the number of food treats they get to eat on a given occasion, such as nine M&Ms, twelve potato chips, or fourteen mini-marshmallows. By the same token, it is easier to cope with foods that are not favorites if children are encouraged to count the bites. "How many bites of meat are left on your plate?" Bertram's dad wondered. "Six," Bertram estimated. "I'll guess seven," his dad answered, and the challenge was on. By eating the meat in six bites, Bertram could prove his father wrong. Preschool children like to count their food after cutting it into pieces. A single slice of cheese turns into two pieces, then three, then four, five, and so on. The

excitement of cutting is combined with the illusion that the food is expanding.

A second kind of everyday activity that is rich in counting possibilities is physical movement. Counting as you move encourages children to develop a steady counting rhythm and helps them learn the principle of one-to-one correspondence.

Another activity that allows children to practice their number skills is making a counting book. You and your child can glue pictures or small objects (such as buttons, leaves, and cotton balls) on pieces of paper and then bind the pages together in a notebook. A counting book may consist of various sets that represent the same number, such as a "Book of 6" with six objects per page. Magazines, newspapers, and shopping catalogs are full of pictures that show naturally occurring sets. Or a counting book may challenge children to count objects in different configurations: a circular pattern, a square, a cross, a star, and so forth. When counting these collections, or in any other counting activity, your emphasis should be on teaching the idea of one-to-one correspondence, not on total accuracy. The important accomplishment is learning that one number goes with each object.

A sequence puzzle with objects arranged according to size helps your child recognize the relationships between numbers and size. When you give your child a sequence puzzle, count the number of pieces first, and then talk about small, medium, and large.

If you feel your child is ready for addition and subtraction, experiment with one of the following games:

Show your child that you have two or three pennies in your hand. Then close your hand and place one more penny into your closed fist, saying "I started with three pennies and I added one more; how many do you think I have now?" As soon as your child gives an answer, open your hand and let him count the pennies. If the child is wrong, see if he wants to play again. The idea is to treat the activity as a magic trick, one in which the child can outwit the magician by giving the correct number of hidden pennies.

An alternative game involves guessing "how many are missing?"

Mother: Okay, Gretchen, see how many shells I have lined up?
Gretchen: One, two, three, four, five.
Mother: All right. Now close your eyes. I'm going to take some away. Okay, open your eyes—how many do you think I took away?
Gretchen (counting the holes that are left in the line of shells): I know, you took two shells.

A third possibility is to illustrate sums with the fingers on both hands:

Simon Says hold up eight fingers. Good, that's four and four.
Now, Simon Says make eight a different way—it can't be four and four.
Let's try five . . . and three, good.
Now, Simon Says hold up six fingers . . .

Children who show interest in these addition and subtraction games will enjoy story problems even more. Mental arithmetic games appeal when it is presented in the context of a real problem:

"We invited eight children to your party and we have only five favors. How many more favors do we need to buy at the store?"

"With you and your sister and me, we are taking up three seatbelts. We have five seatbelts in the car. How many more children can we put in the car with everyone still having a seatbelt?"

As we look at the many different concepts involved in an elementary understanding of numbers, the wonder is that preschool children can learn so much so quickly. Children seem to have a natural affinity for numbers. Counting fingers and toes, reciting number rhymes, repeating finger games, counting out cookies, arranging collections into sets, and completing number puzzles are play activities that children really enjoy. As long as we help each child pursue counting in his own way, number learning will be seen as a game to play and a skill to master.

PLAY IDEAS

When you go in an elevator with your child, ask him to push the button for you. Begin the elevator game in a building with two or three floors.

If your child is able to count objects, she may be ready to take a beginning step in learning addition and subtraction. Put three pennies in your hand and let your child count them. Next, put two of the pennies on the table. Ask your child to guess how many pennies are hiding in your hand. In the beginning your child is almost certain to say two because she sees two pennies on the table. After a few trials and errors she will have no trouble guessing. If your child is interested, play the game with four pennies.

Birthday candles provide a natural opportunity to introduce beginning addition. Make a sandbox cake using twigs or craft sticks for candles. Pretend your cake is for a three-year-old. Ask your child to give you three candles to put in the cake. Then say, "Oops, I forgot the candle for good luck. I don't think I have enough candles."

Go through a magazine or catalogue with your child.

Make a "two" book with your child by cutting out pictures with two like objects. If your child has fun with this activity, try making a "three" book.

Plan a family exercise time and count as you do your exercise. Count and jump, count and hop, count and clap. Count the number of times you bat a balloon back and forth, or count ten strokes as you and your child brush your teeth.

A game of "drop and count" will demonstrate that each item gets counted once and only once. Count pennies as your child drops them in a piggy bank, or count blocks as you drop them into a box.

PLAYING WITH FRIENDS

IT IS SHOWN THAT TIGGERS DON'T CLIMB TREES

I could spend a happy morning
Seeing Roo,
I could spend a happy morning
Being Pooh.
For it doesn't seem to matter,
If I don't get any fatter
(And I don't get any fatter),
What I do.

Oh, I like his way of talking,
Yes, I do.
It's the nicest way of talking
Just for two.
And a Help-yourself with Rabbit
Though it may become a habit,
Is a pleasant sort of habit
For a Pooh.

—A.A. Milne

A first step in making friends for many young children is the creation of a pretend friend. This friend may be purely imaginary, or it may be a doll or stuffed animal. Imaginary friends are ready companions, protectors, or scapegoats. Doll friends are likely to be security objects or babies that need love and care.

Fabian had a clown doll that he was particularly fond of. On his first day of preschool his mother suggested that he leave "clownie" at home. "No, I can't," Fabian protested. "He's only a baby and I can't leave him alone."

A second step in making friends is the acquisition of real friends. The exchange of imaginary playmates for real playmates is not easy.

"I don't want to play with Yanick," Allison told her mom. "She takes away all my toys. I want to play with Coob-aboo. She is much better at playing."

Making friends is the crowning achievement of the preschool years. From the point of view of the young child, the best way to have a good time is inviting a friend to play. As well as having fun, playing with peers gives children a special opportunity to appraise their own skills. "Jen doesn't even know how to swim and I can swim fast."

"I want to jump really high, just like Suzy!" Playing with peers also helps children learn how to negotiate. In order to play successfully with other children, preschoolers need to learn that they can't always be the boss. When Allison wanted to keep the shovel, Suzy explained that they should take turns. At first Allison protested. "It's my turn cause I got it first," but when Suzy started to walk away Allison changed her tactic. "We can both be shovelers. I get to shovel one time and then you get to shovel one time." Suzy accepted the compromise and the play turned into a giggling match as they covered each other with sand.

Section V, "Playing with Friends," is divided into three chapters. In Chapter 13, "Imaginary Friends," we describe how children use dolls, stuffed animals, and make-believe friends as substitutes for real friends. In Chapter 14, "Intimate Friends," we look at the basis of friend selection and describe the interactions of close and long-term friends. In Chapter 15, "Playing With a Group of Friends," our focus is on playing in a preschool group setting. We identity different leadership and followership styles and describe the kinds of social skills that children readily acquire.

CHAPTER 13

Imaginary and Invisible Friends

THE UNSEEN PLAYMATE

When children are playing alone on the green,
In comes the playmate that never was seen.
When children are happy and lonely and good,
The friend of the children comes out of the woods.

Children demonstrate a natural bent for creating non-human companions. Among infants and toddlers, these companions range from traditional dolls and stuffed animals to

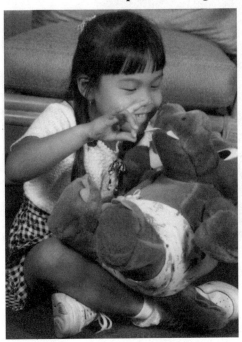

inanimate objects like blankets and bottles. In fact, very young children may form an attachment to virtually any object that makes them feel secure.

By the beginning of the preschool period, imaginary companions have become more than security objects. Now they have personalities and lifelike characteristics, and their role includes helping children act out wishes on a fantasy level or serving as scapegoats. In this chapter, we look at different ways in which preschool children create imaginary companions. Sometimes their imaginary friend is a baby who needs to be nurtured, sometimes he is a peer who

likes to play, and sometimes he is an older, more powerful confidante. In all these forms, imaginary companions represent an important first step in the process of making friends.

PRETEND FRIENDS

The pretend companions of young preschoolers are most often babies. Favorite babies may be either dolls or stuffed animals. New dolls and stuffed animals are seldom accepted as babies without an appropriate breaking-in period. Softness, floppiness, big eyes, and a sad expression seem to facilitate the adoption process.

Many children adopt an imaginary baby and begin care-giving before they reach preschool age. This play, however, tends to be highly repetitive and mechanical. The doll is fed, burped, and fed again. Or, if the child has a younger sibling in the house, he may add diaper changing to the routine. Again, as soon as the doll's bottom is wiped and a facsimile of a diaper put on, it is time for another diaper change.

During the preschool years, care-giver play becomes less repetitive and goes beyond simple imitation. The children actually assume the role of parent and create a parent-child relationship with their dolls. Play becomes highly conversational as children learn to change their voices, depending on whether they are talking to the doll or for the doll. In their role as parents, children relish decision making, deciding what to do when the baby gets sick or acts naughty or is old enough to celebrate a birthday.

Most significantly, the imaginary babies take on the characteristics of the children who are pretending to be their parents. Children create another version of themselves by projecting their own image on to make-believe babies. As the doll babies mirror the wishes and fears of the children, they become companions, for it is easy to make friends with someone who is just like you.

"Velvet needs money in her pockets," Luisa explained to her mother as she prepared to take her favorite doll on a shopping trip. As soon as they got home, Luisa told her mother that it was time for Velvet to take a nap. As she tucked Velvet into bed, she gave her some toys to play with: a Donald Duck doll, a pocketbook, a wallet, a brush, and a bracelet—the sort of things that Luisa liked to play with in her own bed.

When a baby doll graduates to the role of peer, there is a subtle shift in the language that accompanies pretending. Instead of talking about what needs to be done to take care of the baby, children talk about the doll's feelings and ideas. Alyse, Kori's baby doll, aged several years overnight and began looking forward to her fourth birthday. As Kori explained to her mother:

"Alyse will be four on her birthday. She just drinks bottles at night. Oh, Alyse, what's wrong? Wait just a minute. I'll get your bottle. Don't cry, you shouldn't do that."

FROM PEER FRIEND TO SUPER FRIEND

For some children, favorite pretend companions remain peers throughout the preschool years. These dolls and stuffed animals participate in whatever the children do. If the child gets dressed up in fancy clothes, so does the doll. If the child packs a bag for an overnight stay at Grandma's, the doll needs to pack a bag too. The pretend companions even shadow children when they act out pretend themes. "I'm a policeman," Kevin announced to his parents, "and this is Garfield, the police cat." Later Kevin changed to a cowboy, and Garfield followed suit as a "cowboy cat."

With the loyalty of a younger friend, these companions are always willing to play the role of "extra." A child who plays doctor can count on them to be patients. A child who wants to be a teacher has a ready-made classroom of pupils. Debbie used her imaginary companions for a church service. With a pillow on the floor as the first-row pew, Debbie lined up her dolls and solemnly began the service. "Jesus loves you," she intoned in a deep sonorous voice, holding a bible upside down. "Jesus wants you to go to heaven. Did you all bring your lesson books today? Turn to page eighty-four. Now—everybody together—sing. Jesus is on the water."

As preschool children become more sophisticated about the world beyond their immediate family and everyday experiences, the nature of their pretend companions can change. Rather suddenly, baby dolls are replaced by more sophisticated mass-produced toys such as Care Bears, Beanie Babies, Pleasant Dolls, Pooh Bears, and Barbies. Traditional stuffed animals are displaced by superhero dolls, Star Wars figures, Gobots, and Deceptagons. Although the children may have played with these various dolls earlier, they now assume a new importance in the children's play.

Clearly such pretend companions are created and marketed through the mass media, particularly television. Their rise to prominence suggests that children are substituting the fantasy themes of television for the earlier themes that grew out of their personal experience. It also suggests that the media producers have struck a responsive chord in preschool children.

As we speculate about the basis of the appeal of these media-created characters, we can see a difference in the pretend friends that boys choose and the pretend friends that girls choose. Girls are especially attracted to teenage dolls that come with an extensive wardrobe. Boys are attracted to sports heroes and action figures that are fearless, reckless, heroic, or malevolent.

The prototype of adolescent glamour dolls is Barbie, an unchallenged favorite since the mid-1950s. In contrast to doll companions that take on the personality of their owner, Barbie comes with a ready-made personality. As children sort out

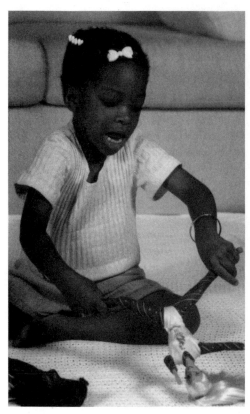

Barbie's wardrobe, fix up her dressing table, or prepare her for a dance, they are projecting themselves into a fantasy role. In a sense, Barbie, with her fancy clothes and expensive possessions, is a modern Cinderella.

While preschool girls use Barbie dolls as the basis for their pretending, the pretend play of preschool boys is most frequently linked to television fantasies. Collections of miniature Power Rangers and superheroes become their treasured possessions. These various characters are imbued with magic power that can keep a preschooler safe.

Hans had amassed an impressive collection of robots, which were his constant companions. One day after a boat trip with his parents, Hans discovered that he had left his favorite robot, "Blackie," on the boat. Hans was completely distraught by this discovery. After two days of listening to his son lament, Hans's father finally went back to the boat to retrieve the tiny toy.

Although miniature objects may serve as protectors, these toys are used most frequently as props for director-producer-type pretending. Kevin, at five years old, turned his bathtub into an outer-space combat zone:

"Vrroom—vrooom—swish—swish—tuush—taush—zp—u—zp—here he comes. Flying through the air. Man the space gun. Four-two-one blast off! Tat-a-tat-tat-a-tat—watch out from above. We're under attack!"

Some parents express concerns about media-inspired pretending. Are girls who play with Barbie dolls buying into

superficial and materialistic values? Are boys who play with Power Rangers obsessed with death and violence? While these concerns are legitimate, parents should realize that this type of play serves a useful purpose. One of the functions of pretend play is to come to terms with situations that are confusing or unfamiliar. Children in our culture are exposed to sexual and violent themes despite parental efforts to shield them. Pretend play can be thought of as a safety valve, allowing children to explore scary facets of the grown-up world at a safe distance. Overexposure to violent themes, however, increases the chance of children taking on the role of aggressor in real, as well as pretend, situations.

INVISIBLE FRIENDS

Nicholas: There it is, Daddy. Right there it is. That's Dooka-Doo's House.
Daddy: Good, let's go in and visit.
Nicholas: Dooka-Doo is shopping at the mall.

Invisible friends like Dooka-Doo are often invented by three-year-olds who have limited access to real friends. These invisible friends can be puzzling. Parents often claim that they don't know if their child really believes in the existence of the pretend friend or whether these companions are just a device for spoofing parents and getting adult attention. At times, children really seem to believe in their invisible friends—when sharing a secret, issuing a command, or protecting the friend from a parent who is about to sit in his or her special chair. At other times, children seem to be quite aware that their friend is an invention.

When Yoko blamed Mouchie for a wet spot in the bed, Yoko's parents detected a guilty smile. When Nicholas claimed that he couldn't go to school because Dooka-Doo would be lonesome, both father and son knew full well that Nicholas was looking for an excuse to stay home.

Although invisible friends are often used as scapegoats or alibis, they serve other functions as well. For children who spend a lot of time by themselves, the imaginary friend may be a companion in a true sense, accompanying the child on make-believe excursions or serving as an audience when the child puts on a performance.

The names that children give their invisible friends are often suggestive of their function. Jad's after-school imaginary playmates were given the name of whomever sat beside him at school. Meling called her invisible friend Ryan, the name of her favorite real friend. When Meling was told that she couldn't have Ryan over, she explained to her mother that Ryan was only just pretend.

Quite commonly, the name given to an imaginary friend is a diminutive form or variation of the child's own name. Jad's imaginary playmate was called JaJa. Carina named her playmate Candy Cue. In these cases, the invisible friend may be a kind of alter ego, sharing the child's feelings and expressing the child's thoughts. When Jad was upset about not going to the soccer game with his Dad, he consoled his pretend friend, JaJa. "You mad 'cause Daddy don't take you to the soccer game? Daddy take you next time."

Singva's imaginary friends were named John and Peter. They lived in the vestibule wall and made their appearance when Singva's parents were busy. Their assigned function was to listen while Singva described his business dealings.

"What a day!" he announced to his silent companions. "I sold sixteen sinks, fourteen ice makers, and twelve bar stools."

With few exceptions, children abandon their invisible friends between the ages of three-and-a-half and four. In most cases, the friends are simply forgotten, but occasionally the invisible friend suffers a tragic fate. Abbeba, who used to live in Allison's hall, died in an accident. Veronica's friend, Noonie-No, jumped into the ocean and drowned. No one really knows why children are so likely to "kill off" an invisible friend. It may be that children are communicating the message that their friend was only just pretend. We could also speculate that the killing off of an invisible friend is the child's way of exploring death and violence.

SUGGESTIONS FOR PARENTS

A child's "conversation" with an imaginary friend can tune parents in to his feelings. When a child comforts his doll on the way to the doctor, parents recognize that their child is scared. A helpful reaction is to talk to the doll, telling it that this is just

a checkup or that the shot will be just a quick pinch. Just as the child is using the doll to communicate to his parents, parents can address the doll as a way of talking to their child. The special role that imaginary friends play in enhancing this kind of communication make them important members of the family.

Because dolls and stuffed animals are so special to young children, it is important for parents to treat these imaginary friends as honored members of the family. Try to remember their names and greet them when they appear on the scene. Make every effort to help your child find a missing doll. The loss of a favorite friend can be traumatic. Statements like, "I warned you to leave it home," when your child is frantically searching for a missing stuffed animal can only make matters worse.

Be careful not to overload your child with too many dolls or stuffed animals. It is harder for children to build up close attachments when their family is too extensive. Identify your child's favorite dolls or stuffed animals and buy accessories for them, such as pajamas, play clothes, blankets, strollers, brush and comb sets, and miniature dishes. When favorite dolls have their own special possessions, children are likely to imbue them with corresponding personality traits. A teddy with a pair of blue jeans likes out-of-door play. A doll with a tea set enjoys having company. As children develop personalities for their dolls, the value of a doll as companion is enhanced.

Talk directly to your child's doll and assume the doll has

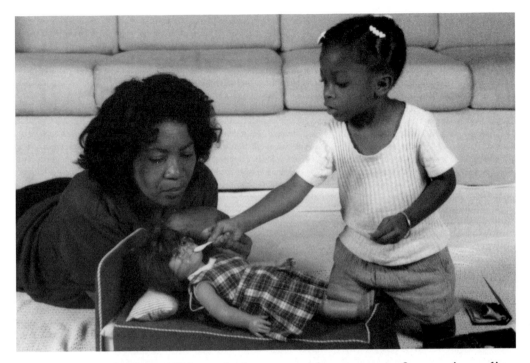

feelings. This technique provides a means for reprimanding your child in a gentle way or for helping your child recognize and express his feelings.

Brenan was giving flying lessons to his stuffed bear, Garfield, and, in the process, hit his sister on the head. Instead of scolding Brenan, his mother addressed her comments to Garfield:

"Garfield, you have not been a safe flyer. You are going to have to stay on top of the bureau until I give you permission to get down."

On another occasion, Brenan had a cold and was not allowed to go out to dinner. Before Brenan could express his disappointment through a temper tantrum, his mother began a conversation with Garfield.

"Garfield, I know how sad you are about not going out to the restaurant. But you know you have a cold and you want to be better by your birthday. Brenan has a cold, too. He is going to stay home and take good care of you. Good, Garfield, I'm proud of you. You are not even crying."

Use an imaginary friend to role-play problematic situations. When Erik put up a fuss about staying home with a baby-sitter, his mother took out Erik's older sister's favorite doll. "You know what? Peggy (the doll) is all upset. She doesn't want to stay in the room all by herself. Do you suppose you could take care of her until your sister comes home? Well, look at that. She feels better already." The strategy worked. Erik was so pleased about being trusted with his sister's favorite doll that he forgot about his objections to the baby-sitter.

If your child has an invisible friend, go along with it. In actuality, invisible friends can spark playful conversations that you and your child can enjoy. Patricia had an invisible friend called Pattymouche who lived in the family car. On the way to play group in the morning, Patricia and her dad would tell silly stories to Pattymouche.

Sometimes parents worry about talking to their child's invisible friend. They see it as a blurring of the distinction between real and pretend. This fear is groundless. Usually, at around the age of four, children dismiss their invisible friends and turn their interest toward real ones.

Soon after her fourth birthday, Patricia said to her mother, "My friend Pattymouche moved to Mount Washington."

As you look at the different ways that your child plays with his nonhuman companions, you will see him building up the skills that are the basis for making friends. Attachments to dolls, stuffed animals, and invisible friends give children genuine experiences with loving, caring, protecting, and sharing. At the same time, parents can benefit from a child's attachment to an imaginary friend. The friend helps the child reveal her feelings and provides a nonthreatening way to handle difficult situations.

PLAY IDEAS

If your child is worried about going on a particular excursion, invite his imaginary friend to go along. This gives you an opportunity to say to the imaginary friend, "don't worry, your friend is coming too."

If your child resists eating a food such as a vegetable or piece or fruit that you feel is good for her, serve a small portion to her imaginary friend. If you tell the imaginary friend that you are sad that he didn't eat the vegetable, perhaps your child will help him.

Tell a story or make up a silly rhyme for your child's imaginary friend. Your child will laugh at your silliness and perhaps create his own rhyme to continue the fun.

Goo-ba-Poo
What did you do?
Did you eat your peas with a knife?
You are the silliest boy I met in all my life.

Do a dance with your child's imaginary friend. Your child will have fun imitating you and joining in the dance.

CHAPTER 14

Intimate Friends

~~~~~~~~~~~~~~~~~~~~~~~~~~~~~~~

PLAYMATES

Oh, jolly playmates,
Come out and play with me,
And bring your dollies three.
Climb up my apple tree.
Slide down my rain barrel,
Into my cellar door,
And we'll be jolly friends,
Forever more.

Celia: Let me have a turn with the pail.
Chen: No way. I need it. You can play with the shovel.
Celia: I don't want the shovel. I want the pail. I have to make mashed potatoes for
dinner.
Chen: Well, I have to make dinner. Go away.
Celia: Please . . .
Chen: "No" means "No."
Celia: I'll be your best friend.

Fortunately for Celia, her bribe was successful. A few minutes later she and Chen decided to make Booka-boo soup and were busy filling the pail with sand.

In this chapter we talk about the different kinds of friendships that preschool children form. While most of the friendships we describe are peers, it is not unusual for a preschooler to befriend an adult.

~~

PEER FRIENDS

Carlos didn't sit next to me at school.
Carlos didn't let me bite his sandwich.
Carlos isn't even my best friend, and he can't come to my birthday party.

Exchanging imaginary playmates for real playmates is not easy. Unlike imaginary playmates, real friends are not always available, and when they are available, they are not always in a good mood. Real friends have minds of their own. Sometimes they won't sit next to you, and sometimes they won't share their peanut-butter sandwiches. On the other hand, real friends with good play ideas are much more fun than pretend ones.

For most preschool children, the bond they share with parents is their first experience with friendship. Peer friendship represents a new step; peers are essentially equals, while parents and children are not. Having a peer friend requires perseverance and initiative. And in the process of making friends with each other, children gain a new appreciation of what it means to cooperate and share.

During the preschool years, a friend is someone who will play with you and, by implication, someone who will share toys with you. Although preschool children show preferences for particular friends, friendship is more often a matter of convenience than selection. Children who live near each other, or who are brought together frequently for whatever reason, will generally become good friends.

Friendships between preschoolers easily cross sexual, racial, and age barriers. At school, Jerome played primarily with boys as did most of the boys in his class. At home, however, his best friend was Beth, who lived two doors down the street. Mavilya's best friend was her cousin Suzy, even though Mavilya was five and Suzy only three.

The most intense and rewarding friendships seem to

evolve within the context of an "extended family." This extended family may be the traditional sort, in which the children of grown siblings have regular contact. Or it may be a situation in which several mothers who are good friends get together regularly with their children. In either event, the children become accustomed to visiting in each others' homes. Because their parents are usually present, these visits are seldom unsettling for the children and the end result is intimacy without tension. The children quite naturally become best friends.

An interesting characteristic of best friends is the ritualistic nature of their interaction. Reunions always seem to begin with the same play routine. Arianna and Carina had been companions since infancy. Their frequent reunions inevitably began with a happy exchange of nonsense words. "Let's go play Seek-a-Peek," suggested Arianna. "Let's play Seek-a-Peek, Peek," added Carina. At this point, the two girls burst into raucous and exaggerated laughter.

Repeating a well-established play routine, especially one that is silly, gives friends a way to get started without planning or negotiating, and sets the mood for further play. As preschool children grow older, they are not as likely to be dependent on a greeting ritual. The children establish a pattern of relating to each other and the play is more flexible and mature.

At five years old, Debbie and Katerina, enjoyed dressing up at Debbie's house. Katerina readily accepted Debbie's suggestion that they play Snow White, and she had no objection when Debbie assigned the lead role to herself. Since there were no other desirable parts, Katerina was even willing to be Prince Charming. Together they lined up the stuffed animals who had turned into dwarfs. "For seven long years, the fair Snow White kept sleeping," Debbie intoned as she lay on the bed. "Then one day a prince came riding through the forest." Katerina mounted the hobby horse. "Quick as a wink," Debbie continued, "the prince unmounted his horse."

"Oops," Katerina muttered as the horse tipped over on its side. Both girls laughed, and the rehearsal began again.

While preschool children are likely to develop intimate relationships with only one or two close friends, brief short-term friendships are established easily and frequently. These friendships may also be characterized by intensity and can help children develop the social skills that cement long-lasting relationships. Brenan and Josh, who had never met before, were jumping around in a crowded motel swimming pool. Josh's mother was sitting on the deck and had restricted him to the shallow end. Brenan's mother was standing in somewhat deeper water watching her son practice jumping. "Watch me, I can do something silly," Josh called out to Brenan's mother. Brenan's mother admired Josh's first silly trick, knowing that her son would get into the act. "I can do something even sillier," Brenan announced predictably. Brenan's mother moved aside, and the two boys started a game of one-upmanship jumping. Noticing that her son's teeth were chattering, Josh's mother ordered him out of the pool.

"But I'm playing with my friend!" Josh protested vehemently. "Invite him to play out of the pool," countered his mother. Josh turned to Brenan, "Do you like Power Rangers?" As the two boys pored over a coloring book discussing how to color the Power Rangers, Josh turned to Brenan and asked, "What's your name?"

The ability to establish peer contact without a formal introduction is common in preschool children. It is a kind of nothing-ventured-nothing-gained philosophy. If Brenan had not responded to Josh's play initiation, neither boy would have had a playmate. The chance to interact with a peer, which so enlivens play, overcame any feelings of shyness they might have had at first.

CONFLICTS WITH FRIENDS

Like most relationships, the friendships of preschool children often go through an initial honeymoon period. During this time, two friends may seem like each other's shadows. Whatever one child suggests, the other agrees to do. "Me too" is the order of the day. Imitative play is an effective way to communicate "I want to be your friend." At the same time, this imitative play involves a low level of organization that makes it easy to maintain.

In time, however, most early friendships become somewhat competitive. When two friends ride their trikes, they race to the end of the driveway. When they swing on the playground side by side, they argue about who is going higher.

Preschool friends may sound petty as they bicker back and forth. "I made the biggest mudpie." "My socks come up higher than your socks." Children, in these instances, are using their friendship to further their self-definitions. Competition serves to highlight each child's individuality. When Kenneth's grandmother remarked about how fast he could run, Kenneth replied matter-of-factly, "I'm the tallest boy in my class, but Jason is the fastest runner."

If peers serve as a standard for comparison, they also can provide support when children feel they are falling short. Kevin was aware that he was less coordinated than many children his age. One day at a birthday party everyone was jumping on a rocking toy shaped like a banana. Kevin finally decided to try it. At the last moment, however, he lost his nerve and began to cry. Later, when the other children were inside, Kevin tried again with his friend, Alexis. In this more private setting, with the help of a friend, he succeeded in making the jump and excitedly called his mother to watch.

It takes time to learn how to make friendship compatible with competition. A beginning point is recognizing that different activities work better with different friends. Michael, at three years old, already varied his play according to his play partner. When his next-door neighbor, Brenan, came over, Michael invited him to jump in the mud puddles. When four-year-old Amelia came over, they went on an ant hunt. When his school friend, Bertram, came over, they went up to Michael's room to play X-Men.

Older preschool children are able, at least some of the time, to avoid conflict by playing cooperatively. Instead of fighting over competing ideas, they negotiate a compromise that allows for shared leadership:

Mason: Let's make a space station for Captain Kirk.
Pierre: No, first I got to fix up the Starship Enterprise. Watch out—here I come. Crrt-u-crrr vrum vrum out of my way!
Mason: No, the Starship Enterprise can't fly yet. He's out of space fuel. He needs to fill up with space fuel. Quick, we gotta build a space station with a fueling tank.
Pierre: You make the space station—I'll make the food tank.

In practice, compromising is not always a pretty thing to watch, but progress does take place. At the beginning of the preschool period, children who are competing, whether it be for toys, play space, or recognition, often attack each other physically. The fight may range from a mild tug-of-war to an outright wrestling match. By the end of the preschool period, most children, at least initially, try to solve conflict on a verbal level. Their instinct may still be to attack, but as long as the fight is limited to verbal aggression, the chances for a compromise are greater. After trading insults and playing independently for a few moments, it is not unusual to see the children drifting back together.

The most serious conflicts occur when children feel excluded by their friends. To be left out of the play is a great insult, for friendship among preschoolers means having a peer to play with. Additional hurt comes when a child feels his or her friend now prefers to play with someone else. Feelings of jealousy run surprisingly deep.

In most situations, exclusion can be attributed to the limited social understanding and skills of preschool children rather than from intentional cruelty. Two children playing together are not adept at including a third party, even if they have no real objections. "When Oliver is playing with Solomon," Oliver's mother told us, "he doesn't know what to do if Nicole knocks on the door. At first, he just stares as if struck dumb by her presence. Then, when she asks to play, he shouts 'No!' and slams the door shut." "I don't think he is angry with Nicole," his father suggested, "he just doesn't know how to cope with the situation."

The complex relationships between three friends are often hard to grasp. "Julie's not my friend anymore 'cause she plays with Andrew," Erik complained to his mother. Like other preschool children, Erik could not see beyond the idea of two-person friendship. He could be friends with Julie or friends with Andrew, but if Julie and Andrew became friends, he felt automatically left out. The possibility of three mutual friends eluded him.

LOSING FRIENDS

Friends can be lost through misunderstanding and disagreement. Preschool children do not usually have this problem, however. Although they are not skilled at making up after a quarrel, they are equally poor at staying mad. After a brief separation, friends who have argued begin to play again, and both appear to have forgotten that an argument ever occurred.

Preschool children do experience long-term anguish when a good friend moves away. Pierre's best friend, Larry, moved to Boston. Pierre's questions about Larry give us a real sense of a child experiencing grief. "Where is Larry right now?" "What does it look like in Boston?" "Does Larry have any other friends who come to his house?" "Can we write a letter to Larry?" At his fourth birthday, Pierre insisted upon setting a place for Larry with a full complement of party favors.

The powerful effect of losing a friend underscores the intensity of many friendships that are formed during the preschool years. Children have much to learn about friendship, but they are already able to achieve a meaningful kind of intimacy. Often they cannot describe this intimacy in words, but it is a formative experience. A considerable number of adults maintain contact with the friends they made during the preschool years.

GROWN-UP FRIENDS

While the intimate friends of preschool children are most likely to be peers, it is not unusual for a preschool child to develop a close friendship with an adult who is not his or her parent. The special quality of this type of adult friendship stems from the fact that the adult has the opportunity to play at being a child. The fact that both parties recognize the pretext does not de-

tract from the fun. As we listen in on the conversation of three-year-old Nicholas and his Aunt Patti, we can catch the flavor of their special relationship:

Aunt Patti: I'd like some orange juice. Would you squeeze me some orange juice, please?

Nicholas (picking up an orange block): Here's your orange juice. I made it.

Aunt Patti: Watch out for the seeds. You better strain my orange juice. The seeds make me choke.

Nicholas: I already strained it.

Aunt Patti: Great, now we can plant the seeds and grow an orange tree. There, I planted one. Would you water it, please?

Nicholas: Okay.

Aunt Patti: But what did you do with the rind?

Nicholas: What's a rind?

Aunt Patti: The outside part. We have to dip it in chocolate to make candy.

SUGGESTIONS FOR PARENTS

For almost all parents of preschool children, their child's ability to make friends is a primary concern. In part, this can be attributed to the recognition that friendships are an important indicator of a well-adjusted child. In part, this concern is related to recollections of their own childhoods. All of us, at some time during our childhood, felt the pain of rejection by the peer group, or the loneliness of losing a friend. It is quite natural to be concerned about our preschooler's feelings, even if their rejection by the peer group or their quarrel with a friend is only a trivial incident. Fortunately, there are many ways to help children with their friend-making and friend-keeping skills without overreacting:

- Model friendship skills for your child. When you invite a friend to your house, talk with your child about the sorts of things that you can do to make your friend feel welcome.

- Provide your child with opportunities to play with other children. If you have an extended family, seek out opportunities for cousins to play together.
- Have a few toys out that invite cooperative play, such as paper and crayons, modeling clay, a few simple puzzles, and miniature animals, characters, cars, and trucks.
- Help your youngster invite playmates to your house. Be available when your child is playing with a friend, but do not take over the play.
- Find out from the child's parents what she would prefer as a snack and invite your child to help prepare it. Save snack time for a moment when there is a lull in the play.
- Do not expect the children to put the toys away without help. Before the child goes home, arrange a clean-up time. Join in the cleaning up and make sure to make it fun.
- Provide your child with opportunities to learn about sharing.
- Assure your child that sharing a toy with a friend does not mean that the child can take the toy home.
- Help your child choose a "share toy" that will not break or get used up.
- Buy or collect toys for your child that are especially good for sharing, such as construction sets, imaginative play materials, and large outdoor play equipment.
- Model sharing in your everyday interactions with your child. "This roll is delicious. Would you like me to share it with you?"
- Give your child opportunities to share. "I would really like a taste of your watermelon sherbet. Thank you for being such a good sharer."
- Play games with your child that involve taking turns.

While parents of young preschool children are apt to be concerned about their child's learning to play with other children, parents of older preschool children may be more concerned about their extremes of assertiveness. Some children are naturally assertive and will win their way in a conflict even if it requires shoving, shouting, pushing, or hitting. Other children are just the opposite. They handle a conflict by running away, ignoring it, or crying to an adult for help.

Parents differ in how assertive they would like their children to be, and no parent is happy with a child on either end of the spectrum. If you feel that your child falls on the bully end of the spectrum, you may want to invite slightly older children over to play. Plan an activity that will minimize opportunities for conflict, such as putting together puzzles, pasting collages, and rolling out modeling clay. After the play session, talk about how much fun it was and how nicely your child shared. Gradually introduce longer play sessions, with your child participating in the planning.

Other children tend to be too passive. One way to deal with the situation is to teach the passive child how to protect himself with strong words: "Let go of that toy. I had it first." "Stop pulling my hair. It hurts and I don't like it." It is also a good idea to help your child realize the importance of not overreacting. When a victim cries and screams, the bully-type child is more likely to strike again.

Another way to help a too-passive child is to arrange opportunities for quiet play with a slightly younger friend. The confidence your child will gain with a younger friend will carry over into situations with peers.

One of the most effective ways to help children develop appropriate social skills is to read stories about friendship. Stories about fictional animals who have difficulties with their friends are certainly easy to find. If you like to tell stories, you may want to arrange an imaginary conflict between your child's dolls or stuffed animals. Perhaps the baby doll could bully the teddy bear, and you and your child could find a good way to solve the problem.

As we look at the friend-making capacity of preschool children, we realize that the development of intimate friendships is one of the most important challenges they face. As children engage in sustained play with a peer, they are able to recognize and measure their own capabilities. At the same time, children are learning about sharing, compromising, and fairness, and are finding out ways to promote play ideas. Most importantly, they are learning about their own need and capacity for friendship.

PLAY IDEAS

Support intimate play by providing props that engage children in cooperative play. A large box that turns into a playhouse works very well.

When a friend is invited over to play, give the children an opportunity to make their own snacks.

Provide your children with bags of props appropriate for putting on a performance.

Give children a chance to invent their own play games, even if they are somewhat raucous and boisterous.

Keep a supply of 'emergency' activities that you can introduce when you sense a conflict in the making. Art projects, clay, and even a children's videotape work well.

CHAPTER 15

Playing With a Group

GEORGIE PORGIE

Georgie Porgie, pudding and pie
Kissed the girls and made them cry;
When the boys came out to play,
Georgie Porgie ran away.

Veronica: Want to hold my hand? We're friends, aren't we?
Mavilya: Yeah, we're friends cause we got purple jellies on.
Veronica: Let's be friends all day and even after school.

For most preschool children, going to school is a happy and exhilarating experience. It is an opportunity to try out new toys, to paint, paste, and color, and to practice grown-up skills like counting and naming letters. Above all, preschool is the place where you play with other children and make friends.

GAINING ACCEPTANCE

Although most children would agree that playing with other children is the primary purpose of going to preschool, early efforts to make friends may not be successful. As we watch a young three-year-old attempting to gain entry into a preschool group, we realize how difficult it can be. Allison, who has been in school for two days, tentatively approaches the sandbox

215

where three girls are cooking dinner. "Can I make dinner, too?" "No," one of the girls replies. "Go away. We don't want you."

The way children react to an initial rebuff is a good indication of how quickly they will gain acceptance in the group. Some children walk away from the situation and either play by themselves or seek out the teacher. Other children force the issue, even risking a hit or a shove. Still other children gradually and unobtrusively make their way into the group. Allison chose the third alternative. She walked around the sandbox for a while and then edged up to the far end. After mixing and patting the sand around for a few minutes, she offered a sandcake to one of the children. The cake was accepted graciously and Allison became part of the group.

Sooner or later, with few or many rebuffs, most preschool children are accepted into a peer group. Preschool peer groups tend to be small (three to five children) and relatively stable. The group is likely to be organized around a central pair with one child as leader and the others as selected followers. Often these groups have a dominance hierarchy with a nonassertive child at the bottom and a leader-type child at the top.

DEVELOPING A SOCIAL STYLE

In a typical preschool classroom, there are different types of leader and follower roles associated with group play. The most visible is the leader-type child. The leader-type child is the director of a pretend family. Ordinarily, the director takes the part of mother. As mother of the family, she selects the space in which to play and controls the props. The roles of big sister, big brother, husband, or baby are assigned to her faithful followers. As we watch these directors in action, two aspects of their behavior stand out. First, they are very verbal children who are skilled in giving orders. Second, they are so busy giving out orders that they may not be having much fun.

Although being the mother of a family is a favorite role, especially for girls, preschool directors take on other roles that command the respect of their underlings. Desirable roles for directors include doctor, police chief, and superhero. Here is director Dennis playing the role of paramedic:

Dennis: Get the bandage! Get the needles! Can't you see he's bleeding. No—not that one—it's too small. Hurry, man, we need medicine, we need pills. Who has the Band-Aid? We got to operate! Hold him down! He's wiggling!
Jordan: Here, I got you a knife. Does he need sleeping stuff?

A second preschool leadership type is the teacher-helper. In contrast to directors, who surround themselves with a group of faithful followers, the teacher-helper child enjoys intimate play with one or two other children. The salient characteristic of the teacher-helper is their reliance on reason and persuasion and their ability to moderate quarrels:

Erik: I want to be the cashier.
Peter: No, you were last time. It's my turn.
Andrew (a teacher-helper): This store is big. It needs two cashiers.

A third leadership style that is seen somewhat less frequently is the "monarch." The monarch's style is distinctly different from either the director or the teacher-helper. Monarchs are the leaders of large, casual groups. They are more interested in entertaining the group than in getting their ideas accepted. Most monarchs are good-natured, self-confident, and loaded with energy. Their goal is having a good time. Although they may get loud and boisterous, their intentions are never aggressive. Often, they are able to use their good spirits and sense of humor to turn a potential conflict into a harmless game.

A group of preschool children were collected on the playground quarreling over a hoop. The teacher was about to intervene when Carlos arrived on the scene and pulled the hoop out of everyone's hands. Seconds later, the group had turned into a train of wild circus animals leaping through the burning ring that "Carlos, the Great Ring Master" was holding in the air.

An interesting characteristic of the three leader types is that each has a preferred kind of play. Teacher-helpers like intimate play where they can use their verbal skills to good advantage. Directors enjoy actor-type pretend play with five or six faithful followers. When there are too few children, they can't exercise enough authority, and with too many they worry about losing control. Monarchs, who are not at all concerned about keeping things under control, enjoy playing with large groups.

They love rough-and-tumble play, and the more children who join the group, the happier they are.

The most common role that preschool children assume is the role of follower. Followers are likely to select a play group because they like the style of the leader. Although a follower is free to move from group to group, he is likely to gravitate to one particular kind of group. The shyest followers enjoy intimate play with a teacher-helper as leader. Children who enjoy pretend play will select a medium-size group with a director as leader. Children who like more active, wild play are likely to follow a monarch. Followers are usually popular and satisfied with their social status.

Some preschool children do not fall into either follower or leader classifications. First, there are the versatile children who are equally successful as leaders or followers. They are assertive enough to take the lead when they have a good play idea, and flexible enough to follow a leader when it appears desirable. Davita was playing the part of big sister in a pretend family group with Rosita as director-mother. When Rosita was called away by the teacher, Davita took over the director role. "It's all right children. Mother will be back in a few minutes. We'll roll out the pancakes for dinner."

A relatively common social style that cannot be classified as leader or follower is the vassal type. These children are subservient to a selected leader and bossy toward other children within the group. Because they are vulnerable from two sides, vassals are under a lot of stress. On the one hand, their chosen leader could desert them and go off with another playmate. On the other hand, another underling could come along and take over the role of faithful servant. Vassals are likely to be aggressive with children who try to play up to their leader.

Assuming a leadership role in a preschool dominance hierarchy is not necessarily equated with social success or popularity. Some of the more popular children in a preschool are followers rather than leaders. Other children who are well liked by their peers have a flexible social style. Even children who play alone much of the time may be liked by the group. The children who are likely to face rejection are the bolder children who have difficulty with sharing and controlling their impulses and the insecure children who do a lot of whining and crying.

GAME PLAY

With four- and five-year-olds, the games that children play together may have complicated rules. A game may involve jumping off the second stair in a silly position or jumping over the poison rocks as you race around the playground. Children who violate a rule may be shouted at, but the game goes on with a full complement of players. Even though the rules of older preschoolers are more complex, they serve the same purpose as the rules of the younger preschooler. Children are eager to use rules because they find they are a way to keep the game going.

The concept of using rules to enhance competition or as a way of assuring fairness eludes preschool children. When preschoolers mimic the competitive games of older children, they are likely to use the rules to make themselves the winner. Here is Cynthia playing checkers with her doll: "Okay, Donna Kate, you get the black pieces and I get the red ones. Now it's my turn. I take the black pieces. Your turn. Good jump. I take the red pieces. This is a good game."

SUGGESTIONS FOR PARENTS

Although parents and children alike recognize the social value of a good preschool experience, entering a preschool for the first time can be scary. The initial task that parents have is to select an appropriate preschool. The second task is to help the child separate from home and gain acceptance in the peer group.

There are many criteria that parents use in selecting a preschool, and it is always difficult to find a school that meets every criteria. For parents who place a high priority on social skills, it is important to seek out a preschool where this priority

222

is shared. A school's concern with social development is reflected in the selection of teachers, the curriculum objectives, and the physical layout of the classroom and the playground.

The teacher plays a critical role in establishing a good classroom climate where children play well together. An effective teacher maintains control without being restrictive. She sets classroom rules in advance to minimize the potential of conflict and intervenes in a nonpunitive way when a conflict arises. At the same time, she recognizes and values different social styles, helping children achieve success with their self-chosen style. Finally, an effective teacher models social skills in her respectful interactions with children, fellow staff, and parents.

The physical layout of the classroom and playground in a quality preschool reflects a concern with social-skill development. Small, enclosed play spaces are set up to encourage intimate play, while housekeeping corners, play structures, and playhouses are provided to encourage the formation of family groups. The availability of an assortment of props facilitates cooperative pretending.

The curriculum of a preschool, like the physical layout, should reflect a concern for the development of social skills. Time should be set aside every day for both free and organized play. During free-play periods, children should have the freedom to choose their own friends and find their own play spaces. During organized play, the teacher should take the lead in initiating group activities. As much as possible, these games and activities should promote cooperation rather than competition. In a running activity, for instance, the challenge could be to run across the length of the playground holding hands, rather than to win the race.

Once parents have selected an appropriate preschool for their child, the next goal may be to help their child separate from home with as little anxiety as possible. Some parents feel that the best method for handling the initial separation is to go cold turkey. They drop their child off at preschool and, as quickly as they can manage it, exit from the scene. With this approach, children are likely to have severe crying spells for a couple of days and then be fine. A second approach is to stay with the child at school until the child is ready to say good-bye. This method cuts down on the crying, but the adjustment may take a little longer to accomplish.

Whether you choose the cold-turkey or the slow-and-easy approach to leave-taking makes little difference in the long run. What does make a difference is the way that you manage the leave-taking process. Here are some guidelines suggested by experienced teachers:

- Tell your child when you are leaving.
- Kiss him or her good-bye in a matter-of-fact way without prolonging the kiss.
- Demonstrate your confidence in the teacher by a complimentary statement. For example, "It looks as if you have made plans for a fun day."
- Give your child a concrete way to know when you are coming back (such as "right after good-bye, circle") and be there exactly on time.
- Once you have said good-bye, do not turn around.

Overcoming the separation problem is one concern. The next concern may well be peer acceptance. When children come home from preschool complaining that nobody wants to play with them, think back to your own childhood and empathize with your child. Almost every child experiences some rejection before gaining group acceptance. We can't fully protect our children from these rejections, but we can provide some help. Again, here are some suggestions made by experienced teachers:

- Be sure to get your child to school on time. Children are likely to make plans to play together when they first arrive in school. The child who is late is at a disadvantage.
- Greet the other children in class by name and think of something nice to say to each child. This is a good way to model friendship skills and to help your child gain group acceptance.
- Look at what the other children are wearing and try to dress your child a similar way. The child who comes to school in a fancy dress when everyone else is wearing shorts can find herself ostracized.
- When you pick up your child after school, try not to be late. You do not want to miss the opportunity of helping your child say goodbye to his friends.
- Don't keep asking your child whom she played with each day. You may be pressuring her to make friends before she is ready.
- Whenever possible, arrange after-school exchange visits with other children. It is easier to make friends with one child at a time.
- If your child comes home upset about something someone did or said, listen to her gripe but do not make too much of it. Remember how short-lived preschoolers' quarrels can be.

A final common worry that parents have is that their child will be a problem in school. One parent whose child was having a hard time described her communications with the teacher. "I know what the teacher is going to say before I even pick up the phone," she confided. "'Your Arianna looks so sweet and gentle, but she keeps beating up on the other children.'"

Despite the best efforts of parents, some children take longer than others to learn the social conventions of preschool. Children who are used to being listened to at home may have difficulty with the noncompliance of their peers. Children who have treasured their possessions may have problems with sharing. In these situations, the most effective rule of thumb is to avoid being confrontational with the teacher. When you and your child's teacher recognize that you have a shared concern, it is easier to talk about solutions.

Whether the period of adjustment is short or long, preschool is the place where children learn how to be a part of a group, how to initiate friendships, and how to handle social rebuffs. It is the place where children learn to read social cues and conform to social mores, where they develop their own social styles as leaders or as followers. Most important, in preschool children develop long-lasting friendships with their peers and experience the fun and security of being a part of a group.

PLAY IDEAS

Use puppet play to help your child develop social skills. Tune into your child's problems or concerns and act out a puppet show where a puppet copes with the same problems and finds appropriate solutions.

Invite your child's class to a birthday party. Rather than bringing in an entertainer, put out a variety of play activities that the children can play with, such as bubble blowing, modeling clay, shaving cream, giant posters with different color markers, dress-up clothes, strips of paper for making paper trains, balloons, and large rubber balls.

Get the children to participate in preparing the party food. They will enjoy decorating cupcakes, making sandwiches, and creating their own sodas or sundaes.

At school provide outdoor props that encourage children to play together: outdoor playhouses, jungle gyms, wagons, bicycles for two, balls, ropes, and hoops.

WAYS OF PLAYING

The child told us through his play,
though not a word was said.
A monster with big scary teeth,
lived underneath his bed.
He built a castle out of blocks,
and dubbed himself a knight.
The monster with big scary teeth,
was banished out of sight.

Thomas and his mother were driving to the mall. Thomas was zooming his play car up the back of his mother's seat.

Mother (attempting to distract him): What would you like to give your sister for her birthday?

Thomas: Three ice cream bars and three horns for her head that turn into boxes and long hair down to her feet.

Whether they are deadly serious or joking around, preschool children have the capacity to break away from the conventional and produce a creative and sometimes startling effect. Thomas's projected birthday gift for his sister combines his negative assessment of what she deserves with his recognition of what she wants.

In this section, "Ways of Playing," we explore different facets of play that make each child unique. Chapter 16, "Play Acting," describes ways in which children act out imaginary roles and design miniature landscapes. Chapter 17, "Creative Play," describes ways in which children express their artistic talents with different media. Chapter 18, "Play Choices," portrays the different play styles of children and parents, and identifies ways these play styles are reflected in pretend and creative play.

CHAPTER 16

Play Acting

~~~~~~~~~~~~~~~~~~~~~~~~~~~~~~

PIRATE STORY

Three of us afloat in the meadow by the swing,
Three of us aboard in the basket on the lea.
Winds are in the air, they are blowing in the spring,
And waves are on the meadow like the waves there are at sea.
Where shall we adventure, to-day that we're afloat
Wary of the weather and steering by a star?
Shall it be to Africa, a-steering of the boat,
To Providence, or Babylon, or off to Malabar.
Hi! but here's a squadron a-rowing on the sea—
Cattle on the meadow a-charging with a roar!
Quick, and we'll escape them, they're as mad as they can be,
The wicket is the harbor and the garden is the shore.

—Robert Louis Stevenson

Luisa: I'll be the mommy and you be the little girl. We go on a picnic. Now you sit
down.
Mother: Is this where we're having the picnic?
Luisa: Yes, watch out for bugs. You want some milk?
Mother: Oh. I'd love some. This milk is delicious. What else are we going to eat?
Luisa: You see any bugs? Don't let the bugs bite you.
Mother: I'd like some dessert.
Luisa: I got some birthday cake. I cut you some?
Mother: Sounds good, but how about a cup of cocoa?
Luisa: Soon you get cocoa, I'm colding it. Let's sing Happy Birthday.

231

The challenge in play acting is to develop a script to keep the action going. Luisa, a talkative three-year-old, moves the play forward by conversing with her mother. During the preschool years, there is a dramatic increase in children's ability to elaborate roles and sequence events through language. Language enables children to assign roles, resolve disputes, and redirect the pretending. It is an interactive process in which one comment leads to another and new ideas emerge to everyone's surprise.

Listening to the brief conversation between Luisa and her mother, we can see three themes that stand out in the playacting of preschool children. First, there is the theme of "belonging to a family." Luisa is playing with her place in the family by reversing roles with her mother. Second, there is the theme of fulfilling wishes. Luisa's picnic turns out to be a birthday party and the main course a cake. The third theme is feeling powerful, and in a pretend play scenario, children face danger with impunity and get their fears under control. In the picnic scene danger never materializes. The scary bugs do not arrive. If they had, however, we can be sure Luisa would have dispatched them triumphantly. We can learn a great deal about the world of the preschooler by looking closely at each of these themes in their playacting.

FAMILY PLAY

Like Luisa, preschool children often reverse roles with their parents in pretend play. Parents can enjoy acting like demanding children just as much as children enjoy being bossy parents. Still, parents may wonder at times, "Do I really sound that nasty?" Probably not, at least most of the time, for preschoolers tend to exaggerate their authority as they pretend to be parents. Part of what is going on is the natural capacity to enjoy acting

angry or petulant. Whether parent or child, it is fun to release
mild hostility without suffering any real consequences. Addi-
tionally, young children may act overbearing to compensate for
their lack of real power in the family. Being the powerful center
of an imaginary family makes it easier to accept a place that is
without much power in the real family.

For some preschool children, the family issue of greatest concern is not differences in power between parents and children, but the differences in the way parents relate to their younger and older children. "I want my bottle," four-year-old Danny told his dad as he sat on his father's lap. "Gosh, did I forget your feeding time?" his father asked. "Here's your bottle." Danny reached out to accept the imaginary bottle and then pretended to drink it by noisily gurgling and smacking his lips. "Time to burp you," his father soon said. Not to be outdone by Danny's caricature of eating, he held Danny horizontally away from his body and then flung him upright over his shoulder. "Burp, baby" was the command, and after several more violent jiggles on dad's part and hiccupy giggles on Danny's part, the baby was put down to crawl around for a while.

Seeing a preschooler revert to a baby role may bother parents because it seems regressive. But in most cases, simply expressing the desire to be a baby helps children go on to accept their more grown-up position in the family. Danny's dad facilitated this development by making the pretend play lighthearted. Turning the feeding ritual into a joke, but still one with lots of physical intimacy, brought the play to a natural ending point and highlighted the difference between real and pretend. Reducing the intensity of a pretend theme through humor is much more effective than trying to suppress the pretending altogether. As Danny's dad admitted, there are, of course, times when he doesn't feel very playful; he then tries to direct Danny's attention elsewhere.

A special family role that combines the power of a parent with the attention of a baby is the role of entertainer. This role might be called "the special child." Instead of growing older and more powerful, or younger and more dependent, the child stays the same age but puts on a special performance. The performance may be uncomplicated: Suzy hopped around the house and turned into a bunny. Pierre threw himself on the floor and turned into a vacuum cleaner that sucked up imaginary garbage. The major goal in this kind of play is to gain the attention of an audience.

Kevin's pretending was more elaborate. His favorite activity was staging shows for his family. Preparations for his performances included putting together outlandish costumes, posting the next performance on the marquee outside his room, and

setting up a row of chairs for his audience. With the versatility of a true showman, Kevin was costume designer, stage director, and playwright. He also acted out every part.

"Tonight you will see the great X-Men, and Juggernaut, and Mad Needles, and Mad Needles's brother, and the other Mad Needles, and Marble, and maybe you'll see Storm."

As children grow older, their interest shifts from playacting at home with the family to playacting with the peer group. As would be expected, peer group play is likely to be organized around family themes. When Cassandra took the part of mother on the school playground, the issue of dominance came through loud and clear.

"Do up your seat belt," Cassandra told Katie in a loud, strident voice. "We are not playing policeman—I am your mother. Now do up your seat belt like I said." Katie, who was pretending to be the baby in the family, grabbed Cassandra's sunglasses. "You give them back, baby," Cassandra demanded. "Some babies don't give them back," Katie replied stubbornly, but she did return them. Next Katie started to chew on her necklace. "Take that out of your mouth," Cassandra warned. Arriving at a restaurant, Cassandra and the other children ordered corned beef. "I want chicken," Katie said, being contrary to the end.

A pretend family of preschoolers often has a black sheep like Katie, a mischievous or disobedient child, and the good brothers and sisters. By agreeing to disagree, the family has a reliable way to generate new plots.

Despite the changing role of fathers in America, preschool boys are less likely than girls to engage in family play. They do, however, re-create another family relationship regularly: that of man and dog. Man and dog seems to be akin to mother and child. The dominant boy can take care of his dog by feeding, brushing, and petting it, while the dog can reciprocate by being mischievous and protecting his master from strangers. Andrew demonstrated a clever way to recruit a large family of dogs. Seeing a boy playing nearby, he sent his favorite dog to attack the boy and ask him if he wanted to be a dog too. Each new member of the family then came into the playhouse and was affectionately patted by Andrew. After the petting he was sent abroad to bite and recruit another boy. Soon Andrew and the dogs were playing tag on the playground, running around and around. For the winner, the prize was "a big bone," a block of wood from the playground.

Comparing Luisa and her mother's picnic with the play of five-year-old Andrew and his friends, it is obvious that the interaction has become wilder and less predictable. Even more impressive is the fact that the peer group is able to coordinate several different roles without adult assistance. Five-year-olds have progressed to the point where they can agree on reciprocal roles (for example, those of mother and daughter), decide on how the two roles relate to each other, and work to maintain the relationship.

WISHES CAN COME TRUE

Sitting on his tricycle, Singva roars up to the television. In the process, his favorite stuffed friend, Beanie Bear, falls off the back of the "motorcycle" and onto the floor. Quickly Singva retrieves Beanie and props him on the trike. With one hand on his hip and the other braced against the television set, Singva adopts a nonchalant posture and stares at his reflection in the darkened screen. "I'll take two hamburgers, four french fries, and six Cokes," he decisively informs his reflection. Then, pretending the face in the screen has responded, he accepts an invisible bag of food, mounts his motorcycle once more, and departs with a flourish.

Singva's mother, who has seen this scene repeated many times, recognizes that the television screen is McDonald's. She knows that Singva sees hamburgers and french fries as the ultimate meal. It is a good way to start each morning, driving to McDonald's and making your wishes come true.

When preschool children play act, all their wishes can come true. Any day can be a holiday or a vacation. There are no rules like "eat your dinner before dessert," no restrictions like "that's too expensive," no excuses like "we don't have time now."

The tea party, which probably has been handed down for centuries, is the prototype of this wish fulfillment. The current tea party is more likely to be a fancy dinner or a birthday celebration, but the message is still the same: "Let's have a party." During the preschool years, it is interesting to watch children

expand their party scripts. Jordana started off serving roast beef and plum pie at her tea parties. Gradually the parties became more formalized and the preparations more elaborate. "Have to catch a fish," she muttered more to herself than to her mother, who was sitting on a quilt that turned out to be the ocean. Jordana caught the fish, then got out pots and pans to cook the fish "with sauce." "Be careful of the steam," she cautioned her mother. Then she set the table by arranging play dishes on a pillow. Placing a block on a coaster, Jordana added this "candle" to the pillow table. "Would you like dinner music?" she asked her mother. "I'll turn the music and TV on." Finally it was time to eat the fish and broccoli—plus sandwiches (in case someone didn't like fish and broccoli). After dinner, Jordana washed the dishes by pretending that a cabinet knob was a faucet, dried them with a towel, and blew out the candle.

As preschool children play out their favorite wish-fulfillment scenes, they demonstrate their ability to grasp sequential order. They learn to order events from beginning to end, adding new events in the right places. If an event was not satisfactory in real life, it can be changed by pretending. On the way to Disneyworld, Luisa's family ran out of gas. As she replayed the trip, Luisa made sure this problem did not recur. "We go to Disneyworld," she told her dolls, "but first we need gas." Driving her imaginary van down the road, Luisa discussed other changes that would take place on this visit to Disneyworld:

> *We're going to see Small World.*
> *We're going to ride the horses and ride Dumbo.*
> *We're not going to Haunted Mansion. It's too scary. Those*
> *ghosts scare me.*

As Luisa played and replayed this Disneyworld theme, she re-experienced the good parts of her trip and obliterated the bad parts.

POWER AND PROTECTION

Obviously preschool children feel powerful when their play allows them to act out parental roles, take control of the future, and make their wishes come true. The wish to be grown-up and the desire to feel powerful come together in the occupational roles children play. Not understanding occupations very well, the children often focus on such generic adult tasks as driving or shopping. In fact, if there are any pretend scenes that rival the tea party in popularity, they are the imaginary ride and the shopping spree.

Vehicles are the most prominent machines in our society, and taking over the control of a vehicle is a clear sign of power. Similarly, money is a highly visible symbol of power. The person who has money can obtain virtually anything. For these

reasons, preschool children mark their imaginary rides by dramatic engine and siren sounds, and their shopping sprees by a never-ending flow of money.

The roles of both driver and shopper are broad and filled with many possibilities. Preschool children become bus and taxi drivers, train engineers, airplane pilots, heavy equipment operators, ambulance workers, and postal workers. Children who are interested in shopping incorporate their favorite props into buying-and-selling fantasies. A child who likes to dress up enjoys shopping in clothing and jewelry stores, a child who likes to pretend-cook goes to the grocery store or runs a restaurant. With the help of parents, the whole house may become a shopping mall, with dishes and food for sale in the kitchen, toys and clothes in the bedroom, and furniture in the living room.

POWER PLAYS

In their driving and shopping routines, children become aware of the relative power of different roles. The provider of services, they discover, is more powerful than the person who is being served. Instead of being the buyer in a shopping routine, they choose the role of seller. Instead of being a passenger on an airplane ride, they select the role of pilot. Naturally, once they assume the pilot role, they have to recruit the passengers. "Everybody on the balloon ride," Alberto announced, holding a balloon he had brought back from the circus. "See, there's a little basket under here where the people sit," he explained to his mother. Having justified his role and having warned the people about falling out, Alberto proceeded to race around the room with the balloon.

The power of an occupational role is also magnified when it provides protection for other people. In this light, preschool children are drawn to roles like doctor, police officer, and fire fighter:

Oliver: The people are trapped in the fire.
Father: Should we try to rescue them?
Oliver: I'm crawling in the fire.
Father: What are we going to do?
Oliver: Put them in the ambulance. I'm taking them to the hospital.
Father: What will we do next?
Oliver: Well, we have the dog out and the mommy and the daddy.
Father: Could we go back to the station and have a cold beer?

There is something ominous, though, about the image of these heroes. Fire fighters break buildings with axes, police officers carry guns, and doctors poke needles into their patients. In their pretending, preschool children often mix violent and protective behaviors, indicating that they see the dual nature of

these roles. Pretend police officers keep the peace by shooting indiscriminately, while pretend doctors give alarming check-ups. "Hold very, very still," Bertram said to Thomas as he bran-dished a toy hypodermic. "I have to give you a shot in the eye." Thomas rolled his eyes in worried anticipation—this was supposed to be a routine checkup! "All done," Bertram concluded cheerfully. "Here's a little pink pill. You want to be the doctor?"

To some extent the children may be copying roles they see on TV, where police officers are constantly engaged in gun battles and doctors in radical surgery. Beyond this imitation, however, the children are trying to cope with genuine fears. Doctors and police, even firefighters with their gas masks, are scary people. Pretending to be one of these characters provides not only a sense of power over others, but a feeling of power over your own fears. Police officers and doctors seem less scary if you've already been one yourself.

The dynamic involved in this kind of pretending is magical—fear is magically reduced by taking on the scary role. Children use a similar coping strategy when they act out the role of fantasy power figures. Specific names continually change, but the function of all superheroes is to help children cope with fears. Superheroes are good monsters just the way police officers are the good guys with the guns. They have incredible powers that are used only for good purposes. They can combat the wickedness of any evil monster, giant, werewolf, witch, or robot and can protect you from dangerous criminals, storms, darkness, or wild animals.

The things that children are afraid of are sometimes real and sometimes imagined. Pretending to be a power figure helps children cope with their fears no matter what the source. At the same time, parents who tune in to their children's pretending can help their children talk about their fears and distinguish between real and pretend.

In the following explanation by Carlos, who is pretending to be Spiderman, we can see how identifying with a power figure reveals a child's fears and opens the way for the child to separate the imaginary dangers from the real ones: "Spiderman is not scared of anything. He's not scared of fire at all. He's not scared of water at all. He's not afraid of noise bombs. And he's not afraid of spiders and kisses."

SUGGESTIONS FOR PARENTS

One way you can support play acting is to allow furniture to be used as stage props. Although some preschool children select a back room, porch, or out-of-the-way spot for role-playing, most children gravitate toward central pieces of furniture. Jordana had her "riding couch," which served as an all-purpose vehicle. Singva chose a large armchair in the living room, which at various times was a fire station or a fort. Older preschool children are likely to create their own space for imaginary play by rearranging pillows or draping sheets over tables. Naturally, this kind of play messes up the room and increases the chance of damage. Some families reach a compromise by providing their children with a large cardboard box or by helping their child identify a "pretend corner."

Another way to support playacting is by helping children find props. While too many props can overwhelm your child or stifle pretending, one or two well-selected props introduced during a lull in the action can spark additional play. When explorer Jonathan had hunted down all the lions in the family room, his mother gave him a sieve so that he could pan for gold. A bag of junk jewelry added new zest to Cassandra's shopping expedition. For children who like to use particular sets of props to act out favorite themes, parents might want to provide "prop boxes" for storing each set of props. Although children eventually mix up their props (the ballet dancer might go shopping or the doctor might go out to a restaurant), the prop box helps with the problem of rounding up the appropriate supplies.

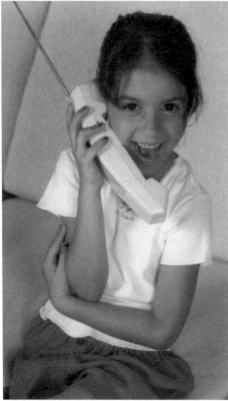

Nearly all preschool children enjoy having their parents participate in play-acting. Young children who are just beginning to elaborate their pretend play welcome their parents' ability to add appropriate dialogue or extend a play idea. Older preschool children are delighted with their parents' talent for adding excitement or novelty to a standard theme.

Jad and Jordan were sailing around the living room on the sofa pillow gathering up sunken treasure. Jad's father sat down on a pillow beside them. "Oh, a pirate's life is just for me. I'll hide my treasure here in the sea, and if any boys go after it, I'll eat them for my dinner." For the next half hour, Jad and Jordan worked out secret ways of making off with the pirate's hidden treasure.

When you join your child's pretend themes, the trick is to participate in the play without taking it over. Adults enjoy exercising their own creativity and can get carried away. Although children enjoy a playful parent, they also need to work out their own ideas. The parent who came up with the idea of turning the kitchen table into a checkout counter may be less enthusiastic about moving the same three cans in and out of the shopping cart over and over again. Another problem arises when the child gets an idea that the parent feels is illogical, such as a stop at the ocean on the way to the moon. In such cases, the parent has to either accept the child's idea or find a graceful way of exiting from the play. The parent stuck in the grocery store, for instance, might suggest that the child continue with the shopping while he goes home to get more money.

Perhaps the simplest way to support play acting is to be the audience. When children are pretending to be entertainers, an audience is a necessity. At other times, preschool children do not require an audience, but they generally enjoy having one. Playacting is not very secretive at this age. An occasional question, or even a smile, lets children know that you are watching and admiring what they are doing. If you enjoy taking pictures, you can capture your child's pretending on film. Your child can later look at the photos and reflect on the way she played out a theme.

Whether you support your child's pretending actively or passively, it gives you a special opportunity to communicate your values. Mason's mother used pretending to demonstrate compromise. She and Mason disagreed about the need for Mason's afternoon nap. When Mason suggested that he was a dog and wanted to nap underneath the crib, his mother pro-

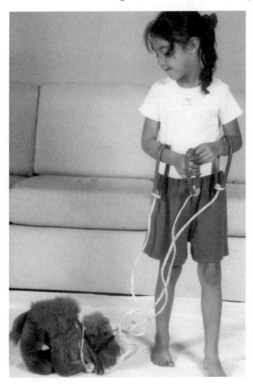

vided the necessary pillow and blanket. Debbie's mother found a chance to support compassion and kindness in her daughter's doll play. When Debbie punished the doll too harshly, her mother spoke for the doll: "Please be more gentle. I promise I'll do better, Mommy." Hans's dad turned his son's gun play into a cooperative adventure. Instead of shooting at each other, the two of them built an elaborate trap out of rope and "poison" in order to catch the bloodthirsty dinosaur who was terrorizing the neighborhood. Because playacting replicates human interaction, it is a fine medium for moral instruction in whatever values parents choose to introduce and reinforce.

Playacting reaches its zenith during the preschool years. Whether children are playing alone, with a friend, or with a group, their most sustained play is likely to revolve around acting. This intense engagement of children in playacting accentuates the importance of the parent's role. Parents can foster their child's creativity and participate in his or her private world by providing the appropriate play space and props, by joining in the play, or by taking the part of appreciative audience.

PLAY IDEAS

Dress-up play is fun. Save Halloween costumes and giveaway clothes, shoes and hats, scarves and belts, purses and wallets, carryalls and brief cases.

Save old sheets. Draped over a card table, they make wonderful hideouts.

Before going on an excursion, act out the trip with your child. Then replay the trip when you get back.

Save different size spindles from paper towels or wrapping paper. See how many imaginative games your children create with the spindles.

Save sturdy boxes of different sizes. They can become tool chests, doll furniture, boats and spaceships, secret hideouts, take-out restaurants, or puppet show stages.

Encourage your child to be the star of the show by joining her in a circus, animal show, or talent show. You might take the announcer role at first.

CHAPTER 17

Creative Play

~~~~~~~~~~~~~~~~~~~~~~~~~~~~~~~~~~~~~

BLOCK CITY

What are you able to build with your blocks?
Castles and palaces, temples and docks.
Rain may keep raining, and other go roam,
But I can be happy and building at home.
Let the sofa be mountains, the carpet the sea,
There I'll establish a city for me:
A kirk and a mill and a palace beside,
And a harbor as well where my vessels may ride.
Great is the palace with pillar and wall,
A sort of a tower on the top of it all,
And steps coming down in an orderly way
To where my toy vessels life safe in the bay.
This one is sailing and that one is moored:
Hark to the song of the sailors on board!
And see, on the steps of my palace, the kings
Coming and going with presents and things.
Now I have done with it, down let it go!
All in a moment the town is laid low.
Block upon block lying scattered and free.
What is there left of my town by the sea?
Yes, as I saw it, I see it again,
The kirk and the palace, the ships and the men,
And as long as I live and where'er I may be,
I'll always remember my town by the sea.

—Robert Louis Stevenson

Kevin, age four, was talking nonstop to himself as he scribbled busily on a sheet of paper: "Here comes the boat and all the peoples are in the boat. And a big hurricane comes—swish, swish, swish—and the waves are jumping and the sharks

are jumping—whee-bee—and the stars are falling out of the sky. The end," Kevin announced, proudly holding up his drawing, which by now was black with scribbles.

For many preschool children, drawing, building, and music-making all have a narrative component. However, these forms of play do not necessarily produce elaborate narratives. The children simply enjoy creating imaginary worlds with their pictures and block structures. Their goal is to design a set, not to produce a drama, and once they feel satisfied with their creations they move on to new activities. In this chapter we describe ways in which children express their creativity through art, music, and computer play.

SCRIBBLING, DRAWING, AND PAINTING

Jordan: I'm making a picture of Fido and me.
Jordana (his twin sister): Me, too.
Jordan: And I made flowers and sun and sky and grass.
Jordana: Me, too. We're good artists.

Like most five-year-olds, Jordan and Jordana are delighted with their drawings. They are not at all worried if the flowers are bigger than the dog or the house. So long as the drawing comes out the way they want it to, the drawing is perfect.

Drawing begins with scribbling as early as one or two years of age for some children. Above and beyond the expressiveness of scribbling—the fun of it and the emotional release—preschool children use scribbling as a vehicle for imaginary play. If their drawing skills are not good enough to intentionally create representational figures, they can look for these figures in their completed scribbles. "I see a duck, I see a turtle," Erik shouted with excitement, pointing to a cluster of lines. "I made a monkey, " Allison exclaimed, as she showed us a group of circles.

Such after-the-fact interpretations are arbitrary, but they do indicate that children are making the connection between drawing and pretending. Once this connection is in place, the children are primed to find images that have meaning for them. Erik had recently traveled from Florida to Colorado to visit his grandparents. Looking at a long red crayon scribble, he saw an imaginary trip:

"There once was a car that drived on the long highway to visit his grandmother. He stopped at lots of picnic grounds and rest areas, all different colors. He saw lots of grass. And finally he got to his grandmother's."

Scribbling is by definition an uninhibited style of drawing that lends itself to experimentation. Three-year-olds experiment with various forms: zigzags, S-shaped squiggles, and rows of parallel lines. In the process of experimenting with different types of lines, three-year-olds are likely to discover different shapes, i.e., circles, ovals, squiggles, and enclosures. Throughout the preschool period, children experiment with colors in their scribbling. Closed shapes provide opportunities to experiment with shading or coloring in. They may find a cross superimposed on a circle, a round sunlike design, or a circle with little irregular shapes floating inside. Such decorated circles are

A monkey

ideal for first drawings of people and animals. By the age of four many children also have learned to include rectangles in their drawings, and these rectangles are especially useful in drawing buildings and vehicles.

REPRESENTATIONAL DRAWING

By four or five years old, many children begin to experiment with representative drawings. "I'm making a picture of me and mommy," Dennis announced as he drew two figures suspended in space with arms coming out of the head.

Once children start to draw representationally, it is fascinating for parents to observe their techniques. Children learn to create different squiggles, shapes, and lines that they put together in different ways to form images. Each of the images then becomes an element of a drawing. The final product may not be realistic, but it is often playful and enchanting.

Another interesting characteristic of these first representational drawings is that the figures lack a common orientation. The daddy in the picture may be upside-down relative to his

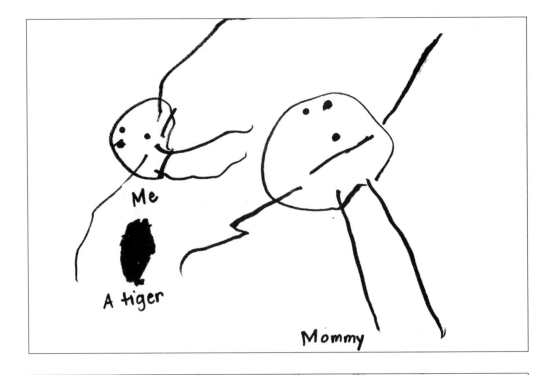

Me

A tiger

Mommy

Oliver.

house, and the sun may be shining in the corner of the page on a clearly rainy day. This lack of a consistent ground line is indicative of the four-year-old artist's step-by-step technique. The child adds elements to the pictures as they come to mind, and orients each new figure according to the direction the paper is turned at the moment or according to where blank space can be found on the page.

In contrast to the spatial confusion between the various elements, each individual figure is generally coherent. By now the children are drawing human figures with arms and legs connected (although the arms might still be coming out of the head). The wheels of the bus are connected to the rest of the vehicle. Interestingly enough, these connecting elements almost never overlap. Long hair on a human figure flies out to the side to avoid touching the figure's body or arms. The four wheels of the car are all fully visible. Young artists seem to follow a rule: Every component in a drawing is entitled to its own space.

The drawing skills of a four- to five-year-old limit the range of objects that can be drawn. However, most children find objects that represent their feelings and ideas. In choosing symbolic objects for their drawings, children seem to be influenced by other forms of pretending. Kenneth, who liked to sit on his throw rug and steer his ship through dangerous waters, drew a sailboat surrounded by sharks. Brenan, who was very interested in outer space, perfected his drawing of a Martian.

EMERGENCE OF THE ARTIST

By the end of the preschool period, many children have entered a stage of intensive drawing. Several factors seem to contribute to this burst of artwork. One factor is that the children are able to relinquish their rigid formulas for drawing. Although their repertoire of geometric shapes may not increase dramatically, children are able to combine these shapes in many different ways. Instead of having just one rigid pattern for drawing a human figure, they can vary the formula to produce different effects. In addition to his square-bodied Martian characters, Brenan, at five, was able to draw a round-bodied daddy, an astronaut in a space suit, and a portrait of himself with very long arms and a chef's hat.

A second factor that contributes to the sophistication of late preschool drawing is the coordination of individual figures into a scene. By five years old, children's drawings are likely to be more sophisticated. Familiar shapes are combined to create objects and people. Ground lines, skies, and suns appear in the drawings. Themes are expanded. Flowers, trees, houses, or trucks are common subjects, and animals are often included in their scenes. Andrea announced that she was drawing a dog so he could smell the flowers. She had some difficulty deciding where to put the dog's head, but as she drew four legs, her dog was easy to recognize.

Oliver and Mason were classmates and best friends. They were happy, outgoing, bright, and creative, and completely fascinated by anything on wheels. As we compare their drawings of a car, it is obvious that Mason is drawing like a typical four-year-old, while Oliver has unusual artistic talent. Oliver's truck is rolling along the highway, its outline is balanced and decisive, and his drawing is cohesive, filling up the entire page. Whether or not they have special talent, there is a consistent orientation throughout a five-year-old's drawing. In fact, the scenes of five-year-olds often demonstrate a pleasing balance and symmetry. This balance is accentuated by the fact that each figure still occupies a separate space, creating a flat but bold effect.

The bold quality of a five-year-old's drawing is further enhanced by an unrestrained use of bright colors. Children may outline a figure in one color and then fill it in solidly with a different color. These powerful, bright colors, combined with the flatness and symmetry, are reminiscent of dream images. Perhaps the drawings of five-year-olds are related, on an unconscious level, to their dreams.

Although some preschool children try to depict action in their pictures, the strength of a young child's drawing lies in his power to evoke feelings. More than ever before, we see the energy of the five-year-old artist going into the depiction of mood and emotion. On his way home from the circus, Carlos drew a carnival scene that had a feeling of festive excitement. Pierre, who was angry with his mother because she left him with a baby sitter, drew a picture of a face and scribbled over it with black magic markers. Celia, following her first experience with the death of a relative, drew a desolate landscape with a single cross in the distance. Christopher, who was a happy, carefree child, drew a field of flowers with a yellow sun in the sky. Whether the emotions they depict are happy, sad, or angry, the drawings of five-year-olds have an underlying air of confidence. For the moment at least, the children are satisfied with their productions and comfortable with their abilities as artists.

Although we have talked about a sequence of drawing skills that children develop between the ages of three and five, the drawings of young children tell us much more about them than their age. Looking at a collection of five-year-olds' drawings, we are struck more by their differences than their similarities. Differences in mood, interests, concerns, and artistic talent make each drawing unique.

THREE-DIMENSIONAL STRUCTURES

Building might be thought of as drawing in three dimensions. In this sense, it is more complex. In another way, building seems simpler because it is very concrete. A toddler who lines up his toy animals on the side of the bathtub is already involved in building. Indeed, building is a part of so many types of play that it is hard to isolate as a single activity. We tend to associate building with blocks, but play with other such media as sand and clay can also lead to building. When children use sheets and blankets to create structures, they are building. When they

arrange objects inside the tent, they are building in a different way. Even children who create fancy dress-up outfits seem to be building as they try on different combinations of skirts, scarves, jewelry, and hats.

In this chapter, we focus on block play because it is the clearest example of building. Keep in mind, however, that building skills are developed with many different kinds of material, including the various types of fit-together building sets.

If there is a "scribbling stage" in block building, it does not seem particularly significant. Long before the preschool years, children name their block constructions and consider them representational. Like early drawings, these block creations are crude abstractions of real structures. A stack of blocks, with its tower effect, may represent an office building or a church. An irregular enclosure can serve as the outline for a house, a restaurant, or a pigpen. By the end of the preschool period, on the other hand, children who are interested in block building have learned to create structures that are detailed and elaborate. Three stages emerge in this evolution.

The first theme that avid builders discover is the power of repetition. A flat line of blocks can be reproduced again and again until the line has become a rectangular platform or floor. In the same way, a single tower of blocks can generate a cluster of towers that look like skyscrapers or a castle. We call this technique "the solid look." Preschool children may start with rectangular floors and then add layers to form solid cubes. Or they may go from a cluster of irregular towers to regular patterns that look like staircases and pyramids.

The second technique, which contrasts with the solid look, involves the creation of internal space. This hollow look can emerge when children try removing the inside of a solid form. Another early version of the hollow look is the arch, a crossbar resting on two supporting columns. Once preschool children discover how to create internal space, further insights follow. They discover that the hollow look can be reproduced. Four- and five-year-old builders delight in constructing a series of connected pens or hollow rectangles. Similarly, they like to build a series of arches, one on top of the other. This multiplication of internal space, in various sizes and shapes, can create an intricate, even a spectacular, visual effect.

Another insight is that internal space can be embellished with objects. Younger preschool children fill their pens with animals and cars; they stand miniature figures inside of arches. By the end of the preschool period, some children have learned to build furniture and other accessories for internal space.

The third and final development in preschool block building is the gradual awareness of three dimensions. Although blocks are three dimensional, children often use them in the beginning as one-dimensional points. They stack up blocks to make a line. Subsequently, they spend time exploring two-dimensional block structures. A series of pens, or a tower of arches, functions essentially as a two-dimensional figure. Toward the end of the preschool years, children begin to realize the three-dimensional character of block building. When they make an enclosure, they want to build up the walls and add a roof. The arch structure becomes a genuine tunnel in which the children plan all three dimensions: the height, width, and length of the tunnel.

These three-dimensional structures combine the characteristics of both the solid and the hollow look. The structures are stable and strong looking, but inside there is empty space. Preschool children are intrigued with their ability to create these secret spaces. They soon discover, however, that this space is not very practical if it is inaccessible. Therefore, as the children experiment with larger and more elaborate three-dimensional structures, they look for ways to create access to internal space. They may, as preschoolers, learn how to create caves and cubbyholes, how to add doors and windows, but the problem is a recurring one. The challenge for the budding architect is to create a three-dimensional structure that looks realistic but still allows hands to get inside and rearrange the interior.

MAKING MUSIC AND PRETEND PLAY

Mother: Fabian, stop making that noise! You are going to wake up the baby!
Fabian (continuing to bang the pan with a soup ladle): I am not making noise. I'm making music!

It's easy to see how all that noise early in the morning would bother Fabian's mother, but from Fabian's point of view he was innocently playing music. Preschool children are enthralled by music. They can listen to the same songs over and over again, dance and twirl in response to a tune, and repeat the lyrics of a favorite song. In preschool, sitting in a circle and singing a song is a sure way to engage the class in a cooperative activity.

Despite their exuberant response to music, preschool children may not be good performers. Fortunately, whatever children lack in carrying a tune, beating out a rhythm, or playing an instrument they make up in exuberance.

"Be quiet," Mason commanded his audience as he banged on his toy piano. "Don't you want to hear 'The Farmer and the Doll'?"

Yoko invited her parents to listen while she played her kazoo. She succeeded in making a variety of squeaky noises which bore no resemblance to music. After forcing her parents to listen for a good ten minutes, Yoko put down her kazoo and bowed to her audience. When her parents applauded politely, Yoko picked up her kazoo. "Want me to play you a really long song?" Yoko asked.

Although it may not seem like it to the parents who have to listen, preschool children are developing musical skills. They listen to favorite tunes over and over again and recognize a familiar song before they hear the words. They love to march or dance to music and to experiment with the sounds of different noisemakers. They are overjoyed about singing in a group or pretending to lead a band. Most important, by providing children opportunities to listen to music, and by applauding their musical performances, parents can set the stage for a lifelong love of music.

COMPUTER PLAY

Children who like to play with blocks and miniature figures can have a wonderful time with software that lets them create their own cities, farms, homes, and amusement parks. Five-year-old Thomas proudly showed us how to build a city. He had learned, through trial and error and with some help from his older brother, how to put in the power lines, water mains, and telephone lines that are needed to keep a city going. But his greatest delight was in making beautiful places, with parks to play in and zoos for the animals, pretty waterfalls, schools, and sports complexes. As he worked, he talked excitedly about all the cool things he was adding and how much fun it would be to live in his city.

Open-ended computer programs allow children to play out their own themes, and preschoolers can be quite creative in appropriating the props that are given for their own purposes.

Arran used the flowers in the storybook program about farm animals as a hammer for fixing the barn. Chen used the characters and props in a story of the Little Red Hen to make his own story about a basketball game. Cynthia filled the page in a drawing program with green, and then used the eraser to cut the grass. Peter added a whole family of kittens to his farm, then made the Mommy find a toy for the baby.

Computers can also be used to make things that can be used in pretend play. Jerome made tickets to his puppet show. Brenan, with some help from his grandmother, made signs for the natural history museum that they had made with blocks and rubber dinosaurs. Caroline made menus and place mats for her restaurant and prizes for her doll's talent show. Nicholas, Brenan, and Kori printed pages of "secret codes" to use in their battle against the "invisible people." Some children's programs provide templates for crowns, hand puppets, or badges. And animated characters can be printed, colored, cut out, and glued to craft sticks to make puppets with which a child can re-enact a story or tell his own.

SUGGESTIONS FOR PARENTS

In both drawing and building, a logical starting point is to consider what materials your child will need. Because each child's interests are somewhat different, it is a good idea to experiment with many materials before investing heavily in any one direction. Look for opportunities to try different kinds, sizes, and colors of paper and different types of markers, crayons, and chalk. Is your child attracted to blackboards, laminated drawing boards, or Magic Slates? What about watercolors versus tempera paint? For building, try colored blocks as well as natural ones, and small unit blocks instead of brand name building sets.

Having provided stimulating materials, you may wonder if participating in your child's play will help or hinder the development of creativity. Here we see a fairly sharp difference in practice between drawing and building. Parents rarely hesitate to help a child get started with a new set of blocks, while they generally hesitate to participate in drawing activities. Some parents are concerned about repressing their children's creativity. Others are worried about their own lack of talent. Although parents, for different reasons, may be hesitant to draw with their children, children are just as pleased to have their parents join them in drawing as they are when they join them in building. They are neither inhibited by a parent who draws very well nor critical of a parent who is completely devoid of talent.

Whether your child is immersed in drawing or building, you can watch for signs that your participation is overwhelming. Your child may continually insist that you do the drawing or building, indicating an "I can't" attitude. Or he may adopt a perfectionist attitude and become overly angry and frustrated by his own mistakes. These signs do not necessarily mean that you have been domineering in joint play. Some children are temperamentally predisposed toward such attitudes and develop them quickly when parents play with them.

The best response is to try substituting peer interaction. As children get more opportunities to draw and build with peers, they come to see that they are not helpless and that they don't need to be perfect.

Parents also can try to develop different ways of participating in drawing and building. One idea is to say that you do not want to play right now but that when the drawing or block structure is finished you will tell a story about it. This approach shifts the responsibility for drawing and building to your child while still offering the stimulation of a parent's creativity. Before telling the story, ask if there is anything else your child wants to add to the picture, any other accessories or miniature props to be included in the block structure. Then, using the imaginary setting created by your child, weave the elements into a story that is simple enough to inspire future drawing and building.

Pierre was working on an elaborate block structure that looked like a Disneyworld castle. When he succeeded in balancing the last of the blocks on the top of the structure, he ran to get his mother. Recognizing that Pierre needed some help in deciding what to do next, his mother began a story.

"Look at that, Cinderella's castle is ready for occupancy! She will be so pleased. Do you know what happened to poor Cinderella last night?" As Pierre's mother continued the story, he listened with rapt attention. His grandiose block structure was even more important than he realized!

Parents who provide their children with a variety of building and drawing materials to foster artistic creativity may worry about the effect of coloring books. Certainly preschool children are not developing their own symbols or expressing their own feelings when they color-in printed pictures. However, if they are allowed to proceed as they please, these printed pictures often stimulate intensive color experimentation. Each part of a figure may be colored a different shade, so that a panda bear has pink legs, blue ears, a green face, and a purple body. A figure may be colored with rainbow stripes or some other design. Even after children have reached the point where they limit themselves to traditional colors, coloring books still encourage thought about color combinations.

Children who are interested in block building go through a similar phase when they try to copy the structures they see on the side of the box or in the instructions. Again, the children lose track, at least for a while, of their own imaginary ideas. If left alone, however, they usually settle for an imperfect copy of the illustrated construction, and in the process, they have experimented with some new forms.

The relationship between creativity and copying is not simple. Preschool children stamp their drawings and block constructions with their own personalities. At the same time, these artistic achievements reflect the visual experience of the children. No one can know ahead of time what new sights will later be copied in drawing and building. Parents can go far beyond coloring books and block illustrations in providing new ideas. Looking at the illustrations in children's books, art books, or even comic strips may trigger a new direction in drawing. New building ideas may come from books that show the skyline of a city or an aerial view of a housing development. Other pictures that could inspire ideas are photos of parks, playgrounds, and plazas, or drawings of medieval castles and forts. With each new visual experience, whether or not it becomes part of drawing and building, parents are helping children to a higher level of aesthetic sensitivity.

When preschool children draw and build they are learning about spatial relations, how to arrange and combine elements so that the whole is recognizable and pleasing to look at. The children also are learning how to express their feelings and ideas through pictures and block structures. They are developing their imagination. These two themes go hand in hand. Children's growing ability to create representational symbols is associated with a growing ability to select emotionally vivid images.

Of course, drawing and building involve different media, and many preschool children have a preference for one or the other. However, when preschool children participate in both activities the parallels between them are evident. Drawing and building are part of a larger domain, the creation of imaginary settings. In a literal sense this is the kind of creativity in which an image is constructed. The broad changes that take place in drawing and building can be seen whenever preschool children try to create a setting for pretend play. Rigidity gives way to flexibility, and haphazard construction is replaced by planning. As the children enter elementary school, their image-making ability matures, and they seem to be riding on a wave of artistic creativity.

PLAY IDEAS

Art

Provide opportunities for your child to engage in spontaneous art. Save a special drawer for white paper, crayons, markers, and other art materials.

Encourage your child to make a collage. Provide tag board, posters, scissors, and scraps of colored paper. Your child will probably focus on arranging the scraps of paper onto the tag board in a way that pleases him. Don't expect him to describe his final creation.

Let your child create a stamp picture. You can use either stamp sets that you buy, or you can create a stamper for your child with a raw potato or carrot and tempera paint.

Children from ages three to five years love to finger paint. Although finger paint sets are likely to include special paper, it is just as effective to use a plastic placemat that can be used over and over. Shaving cream can be substituted for finger paint. Because some children want to save their artwork, it is important to let them know in advance that plastic mat artwork is washed away after it's done. When you give your children the option of being the washer they are not likely to object when their artwork is washed away.

Find a special place in your house to display your child's artwork. A bulletin board or a refrigerator is appropriate. Children treasure their artwork and would like to know that you treasure it as much as they do.

As you take old drawings off the display spot, number or date them and put them in a folder or a box. Occasionally, take out the drawings and talk with your child about the drawings. Does your child remember when she did the drawing?

Building

Provide your child with one or two sets of blocks. If your child uses all the blocks in his set to create a structure, provide an additional set of the same blocks. When a child is given "more of the same," her structures become more elaborate.

When your child talks about his structures, you may want to provide additional props. If he is making roads, give him miniature cars and trucks to put on the road. If he is creating enclosures, you might want to give him miniature farm or zoo animals.

Music

Give your child an opportunity to make his own musical instruments. Oatmeal containers turned upside down can be decorated and used as drums. Tin cans filled with beans can be used as shakers. Pie tins can be used as tambourines; straws with holes cut up the sides make fine kazoos.

Introduce your child to a wide range of musical instruments and musical styles. Play tapes, take him to children's concerts, play "marching band" with a group of friends, and provide a musical background while he is playing with toys.

Give your child opportunities to draw or dance to music. See if she can reflect the tempo or mood of the music in the way she draws a picture or dances. Dance to the music with your child. You don't have to be a great dancer to make dancing with a partner fun.

CHAPTER 18

Play Choices

~~~~~~~~~~~~~~~~~~~~~~~~~~~~~~~~~~~~

BIRDS OF A FEATHER

Birds of a feather will flock together
And so will pigs and swine.
Rats and mice will have their choice
And so shall I have mine.

—Traditional

Veronica: I'm going to be a ghost for Halloween, a real
*   scary ghost.*
Allison: And I'm going to be a ghost too, really, really
*   scary!*
Brenan: Well, I'm going to be a peanut-butter sandwich.

Throughout this book, we have looked at different modes of child play. In describing these different modes, our focus has been on identifying developmental trends that typify the preschool child. There is a built-in danger to this approach. A focus on typical behavior can overlook the sources of difference that make each child's play unique.

In this chapter, we turn our attention to some of the sources of

~~~~

difference in the play behavior of young children. It is divided into three sections. The first section focuses on age-related differences. The second section describes gender related differences. The third section, on individual differences, describes differences related to temperament and differences in developmental status.

AGE RELATED DIFFERENCES

Expectedly, the play behavior of three-, four-, and five-year-olds differs in many ways: the themes the children are likely to play out, preferred play mode, the complexity and skill level of their play, and the dimension of social interaction. These age-related differences are particularly evident in the way that children pretend.

Three-Year-Old Play

> *Okay, Skoo-Ba-Doo, do up your seat belt.*
> *We on the way to Grandma's house.*
> *Vruum, vruum, vruum . . .*
> *Whoops, got to get some gas.*
> *Glup-plup-glup. Stay put, Skoo-Ba-Doo. I can do this myself.*

Whether they are building castles in the sand, serving their parents a make-believe breakfast, or riding a tricycle to the gas-pump tree, the pretend play of three-year-olds has certain characteristic features. Three-year-olds typically choose themes that are pleasurable and familiar: going on a trip, making dinner, going shopping, celebrating a birthday. They gather favorite props with more enthusiasm than discrimination. Rachel, for example, insisted on piling all her mother's shoes in a paper bag in preparation for a shopping trip. They replay the same episodes over and over again, with little attention to temporal order. Michael first blew out the candles and then baked the cake. If parents ask to join in the play, the three-year-old is delighted.

Four-Year-Old Play

Four-year-old pretend play is less rigid, repetitive, and predictable than three-year-old play. Gender differences start to appear in four-year-old play. Boys and girls are likely to choose different themes and settings.

Four-year-old boys need to have space for their pretending. They enjoy playing in groups and are likely to choose themes that involve running around, chasing, and making noise. Often there is an unseen enemy that must be destroyed or a terrible danger that must be averted. Adults are usually kept out of the play and have difficulty following its sequence.

In contrast to four-year-old boys, many four-year-old girls continue the exploration of familiar themes. They enjoy pretending in intimate groups and seek out small enclosed places to play out their ideas. They tend to elaborate on domestic themes and often become adept at acting out roles:

Veronica (playing the part of mother): Sister, give the baby dinner. I got to go to class.
Amelia (the sister): But, Mother—last night I gave her dinner and she spit.
Veronica: When I say to do something, you do it, and that's that.

Five-Year-Old Play

By five years of age, both boys and girls engage in more elaborate pretending. Boys frequently choose to elaborate on television themes. In a school setting, boys gather in groups, shouting out threats and directions, mimicking the voices and gestures of their favorite cartoon heroes. In a home setting, alone or with a playmate, boys tend to play with action figures and Transformers. The boys put their robots through their paces, construct play spaces, and describe the powers and prowess of miniature creatures with extravagant boasts.

The pretend play of five-year-old girls continues to revolve around family themes, with much of the playtime devoted to planning. During the planning period, the girls discuss story scripts, assign roles, choose a setting, and gather appropriate props. Frequently, the planning stage is so elaborate that the play never gets underway.

GENDER RELATED DIFFERENCES

Caroline: I don't want to play with boys. They are too rough and they fight.
Mother: But Caroline, you love playing with your cousin, Terry. And what about your friend Nicky?
Caroline: Well, Terry and Nicky don't fight.

Researchers for years have been studying the differences between the play of boys and girls. In general, there is an agreement that preschoolers, beginning at around four years of age, prefer to play with same-sex peers. They also agree that boys tend to be more physically active than girls and enjoy playing in larger, more free-flowing groups.

The jury is still out on why there are these differences in the way girls and boys play. Some researchers describe inborn differences in aggressive tendencies. Others point to differences in the way girls and boys are socialized. Still others claim that differences in aggression are more apparent than real—while boys are more likely to get into fights than girls, girls are likely to use words to express their aggression. One thing does appear

to be true: Whatever a priori differences exist between the play behavior of boys and girls, these differences are exaggerated when children play in same-sex groups.

INDIVIDUAL DIFFERENCES

Each child's play is shaped by many factors other than age and gender: inborn temperament, position in the family, individual interests, developmental status, and early play experiences. While a comprehensive discussion of these factors is beyond the scope of this book, we would like to describe three sources of individual differences that are especially significant. These factors are individual temperament, early and persistent interests, and developmental status.

Differences Related to Temperament

Bertram was playing racehorse with his grandfather. In the beginning, they were both having fun, but after riding Bertram around the room on his back seven times, Grandpa was getting tired. "This horse needs a rest," Grandpa complained. "Why don't we go in the kitchen and get a snack?"

"No, no, giddyup, horsy," Bertram insisted, pulling on his Grandpa's leg. A game that started off as fun ended up with a tantrum.

A great deal of developmental literature has been devoted to individual differences in infant temperament. Many temperamental characteristics can be identified in the first month of life and frequently persist into childhood. A calm, easy-to-soothe, and difficult-to-arouse baby may become an easy-going preschooler. An active, intense, or easily aroused baby may become an excitable and strong-minded preschooler who requires skillful management. Unquestionably, temperamental characteristics influence the kind of play a child selects and enjoys. An active and excitable child like Bertram naturally gravitates to active and exciting play. An inactive, slow-to-warm-up, and highly sensitive child avoids play situations that are fast-paced and intense.

An awareness of the temperamental characteristics of your child can help you select play materials and plan play activities. Children who get excited very easily do better when their active play is structured and limited in time. Bertram's grandfather might have avoided the temper tantrum if he had redirected the racehorse play before Bertram had gotten so worked up. Parents with a child who is timid and slow to warm up can introduce new and exciting play experiences in a gradual, non-threatening way.

Differences Related to Interests

Although interests are certainly not inborn, we often see children who develop a very early interest that dominates their play. For example, at the age of four Hans had a special interest in animals. He was particularly fascinated by little animals that squirmed or flew around. Out-of-doors, Hans hunted for bugs and lizards. Inside the house, he watched the fish in the aquarium, played with snails and newts, or read books about bugs. The next-door neighbor called him "little cucaracha."

Hans's fascination and feeling of kinship with small living things was revealed in his conversational play. One day his Mother heard him talking to himself: "I wish I could be a slug, so I could go out in the rain puddle. I wish I could be a caterpillar, so I could climb into the tree."

Hans may be exceptional in the intensity and early appearance of his special interest, but most preschool children go through phases when an interest is all consuming. Jerome went through a period where he browsed through dinosaur books, painted dinosaur pictures, told stories about Dookie the Dinosaur that lived in his closet, and built a structure out of blocks to house his dinosaur collection.

Rachel went through a stage where she wanted to be like her brother Anthony. She took over his favorite doll, played with his robots, slept in his "boy" pajamas, and refused to wear dresses. When Anthony brought a book home from first grade, Rachel sat herself in an overstuffed chair and pretended she was reading.

Parents who share a child's special interest seek out opportunities to introduce related ideas. Jerome's father took him on weekly excursions to a natural science museum, where they "discovered" all kinds of prehistoric animals. On the other hand, when parents do not enjoy or approve of their child's special interest, there is a potential for conflict. In these situations, parents have to examine the source of their discomfort and try to find a compromise. Hans's mother felt squeamish about the creepy, crawly things that Hans kept bringing into the house. The compromise they reached was a terrarium. Rachel's mother recognized that Rachel would get over her fascination about being a boy like her brother once she went to school and made friends with girls. What disturbed Rachel's mother was that her daughter always looked so messy. The compromise she reached was to let Rachel wear boy's clothes around the house, but when they went somewhere special, Rachel had to dress like a girl.

Differences in Developmental Status

During the preschool years, children are working on three very critical tasks. First, they are establishing their individuality. They are seeing themselves as separate from their parents; they are beginning to make choices for themselves and to solve their own problems. Secondly, preschool children are establishing their position in the peer group. They are learning ways of making friends, initiating play ideas, and participating in group play. Thirdly, preschool children are mastering a set of skills related to control and personal expression. They are learning how to control their bodies and develop athletic prowess; how to control their fearfulness and contain their feelings of aggression; how to extract meaning from the things they see, hear, and experience; and how to share these meanings using words, crayons, building blocks, music, and movement.

The child who plays crash-up with his miniature school bus may be working on separation and autonomy. The child who is bossing other children in the play group may be trying to balance autonomy with peer acceptance. The child who is boasting about how high she can jump may be concerned about the mastery of new skills. By placing behavior in the context of developmental tasks, parents can recognize the positive side of apparently negative behavior. Then, instead of intervening at the first hint of "inappropriate" behavior, parents can give their children space to play out conflicts and work toward their developmental goals.

SUGGESTIONS FOR PARENTS

Each chapter of this book concludes with suggestions for parents. In these chapters, we describe different ways to tune in to and extend the play interests of young children. In this chapter, we ask you to think about yourself as well as your child. What are the values you hold? What kind of play do you enjoy? When do you feel most playful?

In both direct and indirect ways, the values that parents hold influence the play of their children. Parents who are concerned about violence may decide not to buy their child a toy gun or to encourage aggressive play. Parents who are interested in breaking down gender barriers may buy dolls for their boys and trucks for their girls. Parents who want their children to be athletic may enroll them in gym or swim classes. Parents who value academic achievement may put aside time on a daily basis to read and write with their children.

Despite the efforts of their parents, children often make choices in play that ignore their parents' wishes. The child who was denied a gun may make one out of a Tinker Toy and fire it around the house. The girl with a toy box full of trucks and tools may ask for a makeup kit. When this sort of thing happens, parents should not be alarmed. Most likely, their children have heard their message, but are now they are tuning in to the culture of the peer group. It is important not to overexpose our children to media and marketing images that we find distasteful. But we also need to recognize that a boy living in a harmonious home will not become violent by carrying a toy gun. And a girl living in a home where parents are perceived as equals is unlikely to get locked into the stereotypical female role, even if she develops a preference for "girlish" toys.

In many situations, parental values correspond to their personal interests, although this is not always the case. A parent who enjoys outdoor sports may regret her own lack of versatility and encourage her child to sing and dance. Fortunately, children have an uncanny way of knowing what we really enjoy. When parents have a special hobby or interest, children pick up the enthusiasm and want to share in the fun. This sharing of a genuine interest is a meaningful legacy that we can give our children.

In every parent, there is an oasis of playfulness for a child to tap. For some of us, this playfulness is brought out by rough-and-tumble play, for others by building a sand castle or inventing an imaginative game. Whatever releases this wonderful playfulness, the outcome is delightful. For a few beautiful moments, we become a child with our child.

Credits & Acknowledgments

Grateful acknowledgment is made for permission to reprint copyrighted material from the following sources:

Page 7 Poetry extract from "Kanga & Baby Roo Come to the Forest . . .," from *Winnie-the-Pooh,* by A. A. Milne, illustrated by E. H. Shepard. Copyright 1926 by E. P. Dutton, renewed 1954 by A. A. Milne. Used by permission of Dutton Children's Books, a division of Penguin Putnam, Inc.

Page 59-60 Poetry extract from *One at a Time,* by David McCord. Copyright 1952 by David McCord. By permission Little, Brown and Company.

Page 71 Poetry extract from *Where the Sidewalk Ends,* by Shel Silverstein. Copyright © 1974 by Evil Eye Music, Inc. Used by permission of Harper-Collins Publishers.

Page 123-124 Poetry extract from "Rabbit Has a Busy Day, & We Learn . . .," from *The House at Pooh Corner,* by A. A. Milne, illustrated by E. H. Shepard. Copyright 1928 by E. P. Dutton, renewed © 1956 by A. A. Milne. Used by permission of Dutton Children's Books, a division of Penguin Putnam, Inc.

Page 139 Poetry extract from *Tirra Lirra: Rhymes Old and New,* by Laura E. Richards. Copyright © 1963 by Laura E. Richards; copyright © renewed 1991 by Hamilton Richards. By permission Little, Brown and Company.

Page 185 Poetry extract from "It Is Shown That Tiggers Don't Climb Trees," from *The House at Pooh Corner,* by A. A. Milne, illustrated by E. H. Shepard. Copyright 1928 by E. P. Dutton, renewed © 1956 by A. A. Milne. Used by permission of Dutton Children's Books, a division of Penguin Putnam, Inc.

Index

About the Author

MARILYN SEGAL, PH.D., a developmental psychologist specializing in early childhood, is professor of human development and director of the Family Center at Nova Southeastern University in Fort Lauderdale, Florida. The mother of five children, she has written thirteen previous books, including *Making Friends* and *Just Pretending*. She is also the creator of the nine-part television series "To Reach a Child."

PARENTING/CHILDCARE BOOKS FROM NEWMARKET PRESS

Ask for these titles at your local bookstore or use this coupon and enclose a check or money order payable to: **Newmarket Press**, 18 E. 48th St., NY, NY 10017.

Baby Massage
____ $11.95 pb (1-55704-022-2)
How to Help Your Child Overcome Your Divorce
____ $14.95 pb (1-55704-329-9)
How Do We Tell the Children?
____ $18.95 hc (1-55704-189-X) ·
____ $11.95 pb (1-55704-181-4)
Inner Beauty, Inner Light: Yoga for Pregnant Women
____ $18.95 pb (1-55704-315-9)
In Time and With Love
____ $21.95 hc (0-937858-95-1)
____ $12.95 pb (0-937858-96-X)
Loving Hands: Traditional Baby Massage
____ $15.95 pb (1-55704-314-0)
Mothering the New Mother, Rev. Ed.
____ $16.95 pb (1-55704-317-5)
My Body, My Self for Boys
____ $11.95 pb (1-55704-230-6)
My Body, My Self for Girls
____ $11.95 pb (1-55704-150-4)
My Feelings, My Self
____ $11.95 pb (1-55704-157-1)
Raising Your Jewish/Christian Child
____ $12.95 pb (1-55704-059-1)
The Ready-to-Read, Ready-to-Count Handbook
____ $11.95 pb (1-55704-093-1)

Saying No Is Not Enough, Rev. Ed.
____ $14.95 pb (1-55704-318-3)
The Totally Awesome Business Book for Kids (and Their Parents)
____ $10.95 pb (1-55704-226-8)
The Totally Awesome Money Book for Kids (and Their Parents)
____ $18.95 hc (1-55704-183-0)
____ $10.95 pb (1-55704-176-8)
The What's Happening to My Body? Book for Boys
____$18.95 hc (1-55704-002-8)
____$11.95 pb (0-937858-99-4)
The What's Happening to My Body? Book for Girls
____ $18.95 hc (1-55704-001-X)
____ $11.95 pb (0-937858-98-6)
Your Child at Play: Birth to One Year, Rev.
____ $24.95 hc (1-55704-334-5)
____ $15.95 pb (1-55704-330-2)
Your Child at Play: One to Two Years, Rev.
____ $24.95 hc (1-55704-335-3)
____ $15.95 pb (1-55704-331-0)
Your Child at Play: Two to Three Years, Rev.
____ $24.95 hc (1-55704-336-15)
____ $15.95 pb (1-55704-332-9)
Your Child at Play: Three to Five Years, Rev.
____ $24.95 hc (1-55704-337-X)
____ $15.95 pb (1-55704-333-7)

For postage and handling, please add $3.00 for the first book, plus $1.00 for each additional book. Prices and availability are subject to change.

I enclose a check or money order payable to **Newmarket Press** in the amount of _____

Name _____

Address _____

City/State/Zip _____

For discounts on orders of five or more copies or to get a catalog,
contact Newmarket Press, Special Sales Department, 18 East 48th Street, NY, NY 10017;
Tel.: 212-832-3575 or 800-669-3903; Fax: 212-832-3629.